BEHIND
PALACE DOORS

BEHIND PALACE DOORS

MY SERVICE AS THE QUEEN MOTHER'S EQUERRY

MAJOR COLIN BURGESS

WITH PAUL CARTER

JOHN BLAKE

Published by John Blake Publishing Ltd,
3 Bramber Court, 2 Bramber Road,
London W14 9PB, England

www.johnblakepublishing.co.uk

First published in paperback in 2007

ISBN 978 1 84454 444 8

British Library Cataloguing-in-Publication Data:

A catalogue record for this book is available from the British Library.

Design by www.envydesign.co.uk

Printed in Great Britain by CPI Bookmarque, Croydon, Surrey

3 5 7 9 10 8 6 4

Papers used by John Blake Publishing are natural, recyclable products made
from wood grown in sustainable forests. The manufacturing processes
conform to the environmental regulations of the country of origin.

Every attempt has been made to contact the relevant copyright-holders,
but some were unobtainable. We would be grateful if the appropriate people
could contact us.

To the personal protection officers, who risk everything
and work very hard to not be noticed

COLIN BURGESS was commissioned into the Irish Guards in 1987 and took part in operations in Northern Ireland and Central America. In 1989 he completed the Army Pilot's course and flew as an operational helicopter pilot until 1993. Colin was offered the role as equerry to the Queen Mother in 1994 and finished this two-year posting when he left the Army. Colin has since gone on to become a successful TV producer. He has planned and developed three TV channels and is a leading consultant on Internet Television.

PAUL CARTER began his career in journalism in 1990 at the *Oldham Advertiser*. He has worked as a sports reporter for the *Sunday Times*, features writer for the *Sun* and also at Sky News. In 1996 Paul joined Sport Newspapers and was made editor of the *Sunday Sport* in June 2001. He has had his poetry and short stories published.

ACKNOWLEDGEMENTS

Thanks to everyone who helped with compiling this book.
Thanks to Simon Dean and Ged Mason.

CONTENTS

INTRODUCTION

'She was quite simply the most magical grandmother you could possibly have and I was utterly devoted to her.

'Her departure has left an irreplaceable chasm in countless lives but, thank God, we are all the richer for the sheer joy of her presence and everything she stood for.

'Above all, she understood the British character and her heart belonged to this ancient land and its equally indomitable and humorous inhabitants, whom she served with panache, style and unswerving dignity for very nearly eighty years.'

HRH The Prince of Wales

'During her long and extraordinary life, her grace, her sense of duty and her remarkable zest for life made her loved and admired by people of all ages and backgrounds, revered within our borders and beyond.

'She was a unifying figure for Britain, inspiring love and affection in all she met.

'The respect she received and the outpouring of affection after her death are not the result of her long life. The tributes could have been a ritual, but they were not. They were genuine and heartfelt and from young and old from all walks of life.

'It is the belief in duty that captures her spirit best. Yet it is not duty in an arid or formal sense; she enjoyed life, lived it and loved it to the full.

'She loved her country and in turn it loved her.'

The Rt. Hon. Tony Blair,
Prime Minister

'The Queen Mother was a wonderful queen and an extraordinary person. Her death is more than a source of grief to the royal family. It is an irreplaceable loss to the whole nation.'

The Rt. Hon. Lady Thatcher,
Former Prime Minister

'We each had an individual and unique relationship with our grandmother – she was very, very special indeed.'

HRH The Duke of York

'The Queen Mother was a pillar of strength and inspiration to many people all over the world.'

Mr George W. Bush, President of the
United States of America

'She was an exceptional person who devoted her life to her family, her nation and the Commonwealth.'

Mr Don MacKinnon, Commonwealth
Secretary-General

'Our country is the richer for her life and the poorer at her death.'

The Rt. Hon. Sir John Major,
Former Prime Minister

'She treated people in a friendly way, with sympathy and interest. Many also in Germany admired her.'

Mr Johannes Rau, Former President of Germany

'The Queen Mother was a woman of deep faith and deep interest in people. Whenever a person met her, it was almost as if you were the only person who counted at that moment. 'It was remarkable that a woman of such faith and astonishing vitality, in spite of her age, took such an interest in people.

'I think that throughout her life she had a great sense of duty and obligation to her country.'

Dr George Carey, Former Archbishop
of Canterbury

These are just a few of the many tributes that poured in for Her Majesty the Queen Mother, known affectionately as the Queen Mum, after her death in March 2002. Many tried to paint a picture of a woman who was unswerving in her duty as the most senior of the Royal Family and who was kind, generous, thoughtful and hard-working but above all a very private person. For here lies the great mystery in the Queen Mother's life – it was virtually impossible to puncture her outer shell and really get to know what she was like deep down. Many tried – close friends such as Noel Coward, Fred Astaire, her friends in the Special Forces and her ladies-in-waiting – but nearly all failed.

Type her name into Google and you'll get hundreds of thousands of hits. But nearly all say very little about her, save for a smattering of quotes she has come out with over the many years and the odd anecdote, many of which have proven to be apocryphal, because so little is actually known about her life.

So what was she really like? What made her tick? What were her interests and hobbies, if any? Whom did she like and dislike? What were her views on the French, the Germans, Britain and the Commonwealth? What did she do to relax and what was she like in the moments when she was caught off guard?

These are all questions that have never really been answered, even a few years after her death, because nobody has ever come forward to tell the real story of what the Queen Mother was actually like. People like her page William Tallon or her Private Secretary Sir Alastair Aird all have secrets and stories to tell, but as the days and months go by it's becoming increasingly apparent that they will take these stories with them to the grave. The reluctance of so many of her former members of staff to reveal all is baffling, given the public's appetite for such knowledge. Yet I have held back from telling some stories. Maybe it is because she was such a private person that they feel it is an intrusion into her privacy. But she left such a magic legacy that it seems ridiculous to let the memory of her life just fade away.

Step forward Major Colin Burgess. He worked as Equerry to the Queen Mother between 1994 and 1996 and continued to see her on a regular basis until her death. He worked with her every day and would often spend long periods alone with the Queen Mother, periods in which they reflected on things past and present. Here, for the first time, is his story.

It was a turbulent time for the Royals during the years that Colin worked at Clarence House. Prince Charles and Princess Diana's marriage was collapsing and there were negative stories about the Royals popping up almost every day in the press and on television. Colin reveals how the Queen Mother coped with events leading up to the biggest royal crisis since the abdication, namely the death of Diana. He reveals the stresses and strains of life in the Royal Household, the trips, the official visits and the moments when the Queen Mother and other Royals could relax, away from the prying eyes of the public and the media. It's an amazing tale, that was told to me in a series of informal chats over the course of six months, and which paints the fullest and most in-depth portrait of the Queen Mother, her character and personality, that has appeared since her death. She was the original 'Iron Lady' long before Margaret Thatcher assumed that mantle; someone who lived life with a steely determination to make the best of every bad situation and enjoy the good ones to the full. It was clear from our conversations that Colin had and still has a deep fondness and respect for the Queen Mother and out of this comes a portrait of a very private Royal that goes some way to probing what could best be described as her inner layer.

Paul Carter

CHAPTER ONE

A SLEEPING LUNCH

The summer of 1995 had been glorious. There had been constant blazing sunshine since Wimbledon and this particular day was no different. The Queen Mother was enjoying lunch in the garden of Clarence House with her 'home team': her treasurer, Sir Ralph Anstruther; her private secretary, Sir Alastair Aird; her senior lady-in-waiting, Dame Frances Campbell-Preston, and me. By 'home team' I mean her top staff, the people she relied on day in and day out to get things done and make her life as comfortable as possible. So there we sat – I had no reason to suspect this day would be any different from ones that had gone before, but I was wrong. We had finished the main part of the meal which had consisted of an egg starter followed by chicken and potatoes, mashed potatoes because they were the Queen Mum's favourite. The wine, a full-bodied claret which wasn't really conducive to a hot summer's day, had been passed round and a few bottles drunk, and conversation dipped in and out of subjects as diverse as World War II and the latest episode of *EastEnders*. About five minutes after we had finished our main course, though, I began to notice that the chatter was slowing down, rather like a record meanders to a gradual stop when you turn the speed off. Then I saw Ralph nodding off and I just thought, oh well, never mind. He had done this before and age was catching up with him, plus we weren't entertaining guests or anything so it didn't really matter. But no sooner had he started snoring than the Queen Mother closed her eyes and she was asleep. This was a first for me. I had never seen the Queen Mother fall asleep during any meal. I turned to Alastair to ask his advice because I really didn't know what to do. I mean, what is the correct procedure for waking up a member of royalty who has nodded off during a meal? Did any exist? Alastair was unable to answer me because he, too, had fallen asleep. The next thing I heard was a gentle thud on the dining table as Dame Frances's head hit it and she had gone as well. The four of them sat there absolutely out of it with Alastair gently buzzing as well and the Queen Mother's head slumped forward.

I sat there for five minutes, which became ten, and all the while I was thinking, someone is going to wake up any minute, but they didn't. All in all, I sat for a full thirty-five minutes not knowing what the hell to do. At one point, I actually got up to stretch my legs and go for a bit of a walk round before coming back to sit down again among the sleeping throng. The merest hint of an idea hit me: I imagined what it would be like to draw comedy moustaches on their faces, just as Steve Harmison did recently to Freddie Flintoff during the Ashes celebrations! The whole situation was bonkers. I was banking on a waiter appearing to clear the plates. But he wouldn't appear until the Queen Mother rang the bell, and she wasn't going to do that because she was gently contemplating the events of the day behind closed eyes. Eventually, it got to the point where I felt something had got to happen otherwise I would be spending the rest of the day just sitting there. So I thought, damn it, and I rang the bell that summoned the servants in a desperate attempt to rouse them. Now this was a major breach of protocol. Nobody can ring the bell unless invited to by the Queen Mother. And blimey, as soon as it rang they all sat up and just carried on from where they had left off with Ralph exclaiming, 'And of course the Italians simply gave in once the Germans had gone.'

Alastair added, 'You know I just don't know, anyway…'

And off they all went, chattering away as though the whole of the previous thirty-five minutes had never happened.

I tried not to look too surprised and thinking to myself that, in all the time I had been working at Clarence House, this was possibly the most bizarre moment I had witnessed. But in the end nothing really surprised me about working in a royal household because I had met some of the most eccentric, entertaining and charming people that I had ever met in my life and the opportunity arose completely by chance.

I was about to leave the Army, in 1994, at the age of twenty-six, having spent three years in the Irish Guards. After completing the one-year Army pilots' course, I had then flown helicopters in the UK, Northern Ireland and, finally, in Australia. I felt I needed a fresh challenge and an opportunity came up to fly with the Air Ambulance in Sydney, a challenge that I was looking forward to. But this was to pass me by with just one telephone call from my regimental adjutant. He asked if I would be interested in looking after the Queen Mother. This completely threw me. I asked him in what capacity would I be looking after her? I kept thinking: what does he mean 'look after'? He told me the position was as the Queen Mother's equerry. I had heard of an equerry but only in the old-fashioned sense of it deriving from the Latin *eques*, meaning knight or horseman. But the job had nothing to do with fillies and mares and stables. Instead, it involved being around the Queen Mother for the majority of the day as what you might call her fixer and organiser for the two years that each equerry held the post. The role itself didn't really have a set job description, or any training as such. You couldn't apply for it; you were invited to do it by the Army. I was a bit confused and mightily surprised. I wondered why the hell anybody would want me looking after the Queen Mother; it would be like putting Paul Gascoigne in charge of a brewery or something. I didn't come from a wealthy background and, to paraphrase Tony Blair, I was just a regular kind of guy. Surely the job would go to someone of a much higher social standing than I had. Previous equerries had included such

4

luminaries as Earl Spencer, Princess Diana's father, and Captain Peter Townsend, who almost ended up marrying Princess Margaret. I then discovered that they had head-hunted two other people, both with double-barrelled surnames, and I was up against them for the job. I was sure I was only being put forward to make the process seem fairer; that is, to tick the right boxes in terms of giving everyone from each social bracket a fair whack. The other two were much more what I would term upper class in their manners; at least what I thought that was at the time. They were a bit stiff and a little aloof, things that to me seemed to be necessary requirements of the job and which therefore would make them far more suitable than I could ever be. I had a tendency to crack jokes and my experiences as a pilot, where you are left very much to make your own decisions, had made me less in-tune with the Army system, and had given me a healthy scepticism of unnecessary protocol. But I was invited to lunch with the Queen Mum's treasurer Sir Ralph Anstruther at Pirbright Army Barracks in Surrey and I thought, well, I'll give it my best shot and just be myself. If he didn't like me, then it would be providence and I would simply continue with my plans to fly in Australia.

Sir Ralph, a seventy-two-year-old former Coldstream Guards Officer, was in charge of the Royal purse, which meant he oversaw the Queen Mother's spending, and was feared by all the staff at Clarence House because he was a stickler for the rules and vigorously enforced them. I think it all stemmed from his time in the Second World War. He had fought in the Second Battalion that landed in Algiers in 1942. Some months later, in 1943, his company attacked an enemy stronghold north east of El Aroussa in Tunisia, nicknamed 'Steamroller Farm'. As they approached in Churchill tanks, Anstruther and his men had to march the last mile towards the enemy on foot and exposed to intense enemy fire. It became obvious to him that the battalion needed cover and, despite being wounded, he refused any medical attention until his men were safely withdrawn. He achieved this with such skill and direction that there were no casualties and he personally shepherded the wounded back to safe ground to be treated. For this he won the Military Cross. But his heroism didn't stop his commanding officer berating him from time to time for not having his tie done up properly or for having muddy shoes, and it was this attention to detail that he had somehow inherited from the Army and brought with him to the Royal Household which sometimes made the Old Etonian, who still called airports 'aerodromes', exude an air of crusty formality that made him seem horribly stiff and unapproachable to other members of staff. But actually, I liked him. He was 'old school' Army, a dying breed nowadays, and wanted everything to be done properly. That's why he went on constantly about shiny shoes and starched collars and having the proper clips and pins. Staff would live in fear of his daily inspections. Even senior staff, including the private secretary and the equerry, were not spared the eagle eyes of Sir Ralph and we would all subtly and almost subconsciously check ourselves over before he came into the room. But, to me, that was how you did things in the Army, so I didn't mind so much. I just utilised the things I had picked up in Her Majesty's Forces and made sure I always had polished shoes and wore the correct apparel for each occasion. One of the few times I did see Ralph drop his guard was during a State banquet, when a young lady waltzed passed him and he turned to me and said, 'Look how high that girl's dress is. You can almost see her crotch.'

I remember thinking, did he just say what I think he said? This went way beyond accepted protocol and certainly was not part of the list of things an equerry had to check out! It was akin to the first time you hear your father swear in front of you in the sense of it seeming rather surreal, and I couldn't have been more surprised than if I had woken up with my face sewn to the carpet.

So there I was sitting across the table from this fairly frail old man, who was dressed immaculately and sported a neatly trimmed moustache, and the other two men up for the job who were either side of him. I thought to myself, they have smoothed themselves into position already and I have no chance. So I relaxed completely and, thinking the job was out of my grasp, I became chattier. About half an hour into the buffet lunch, Ralph discovered that I had an uncle who was in the Coldstream Guards, and that seemed to swing the whole interview my way. The other two candidates were suddenly left out in the cold. All we talked about for the rest of the meal was Ralph's time in the Army and my uncle's history. At some stage during the interview, my two rivals for the job left the table to get some pudding.

As soon as they were out of earshot, Ralph turned to me and said, 'Don't think much of those two. They're far too oily for me.'

I suddenly realised I had moved from rank outsider to front runner and sure enough, less than a week later, I got a call to go and have lunch with the Queen Mother at Clarence House. She wanted to assess my suitability. I was told to turn up wearing a suit and a detachable, starched collar.

I had eaten with royalty before. It was at Windsor Castle where the Royals had converged for their annual winter break – they moved to Sandringham after the fire – and I was invited there as an Officer of the Guards for dinner in 1987 and had sat between Marina Ogilvy and Princess Diana. It was an amazing evening. Diana was lovely, really lovely, and we talked about life, relationships and a whole host of other fairly innocent topics. She really did come across as this very pleasant and extremely charming young girl, and if she and Charles where having problems at that stage, then she hid them very well. The experience was enjoyable, if a little daunting.

Fast forward seven years and in the summer of 1994, it appeared that I was faced with an even more daunting prospect: a mid-week lunch with the Queen Mother who was then the most senior Royal on the planet. I arrived at her London home and was led through rooms containing porcelain Limoges eggs, amazing paintings that were mainly by British artists of the early to mid-twentieth century, antique grandfather clocks and all sorts of grand objects that made you think you were walking through an old museum;

but it wasn't a museum, it was a working house where every morning a clock-winder would come round and wind up all the clocks. I fell instantly in love with the heritage of it all; it was a house that seemed lived in. Critics have said the Queen Mother allowed Clarence House to fall into disrepair in her later years. I disagree. I would compare it to a fine wine in that the more you leave it the more character it seems to develop. It was wonderful, even down to wearing those starched collars which gave me a terrible neck rash for the first year of my employment there, until I discovered I should have worn them one size too big for comfort. With the strict dress code and the antique furniture, it did very much resemble an Edwardian household and this was in some ways a tribute to its history. Historically, it has been home to some of the world's most prestigious aristocrats. The three-storey mansion was built by John Nash between 1825 and 1827 for Prince William Henry, Duke of Clarence. The Prince lived there as King William IV from 1830 until 1837, and it was the London home of the Queen Mother from 1953 until her death. In 1942, it saw war service when it was made available for the use of the War Organisation of the British Red Cross and the Order of St John of Jerusalem where 200 members of staff of the Foreign Relations Department kept contact with British prisoners-of-war abroad and ran the Red Cross Postal Message Scheme. As I walked through the house, soaking up the atmosphere and the history of the place, I just thought, wow!

As I lunched with the Queen Mother in these fantastic surroundings, I wondered how many people got the chance to have even ten minutes with her, never mind enjoy a full and rather personal meal. I kept experiencing moments of sheer exhilaration during which I would be thinking, if only my family could see me now.

The Queen Mother broke the ice by saying to me: 'So, Colin, tell me a bit about yourself. Do you have a girlfriend?'

'Erm, no, ma'am,' I replied, thinking this was all a bit unusual.

I had expected a much more formal kick-off, but I suppose it was a great way of putting me at ease.

'Oh, why not?' she asked.

'I'm just waiting for the right girl to come along,' I said.

And she just left it at that, no follow-up question, nothing. However, she didn't seem displeased. The job was, after all, only given to single men on account of the unsociable hours that included late duties, entertaining and other things. So to have a full-time girlfriend would not have been easy. I felt I had somehow passed the first test. In hindsight, of course, that is exactly what it was, a test. We then went on to another subject and in her own very informal and very chatty way she proceeded to extract all the information she needed while very subtly assessing my suitability for the position. Luckily, things seemed to be going in the right direction.

For the next two hours, we talked of my family, where I lived, my education and a whole host of other personal things such as where I liked to go on holiday, whether I had pets or not, which also seemed to be quite important to her, and I remember her being keen to talk about the fact that I had boxed when I was younger. She also steered the conversation towards horse racing which I knew she loved but which I knew very little about myself, so I told her that I had the odd flutter now and then, which was a bit of an exaggeration because I only betted on the Grand National and I even missed that some years.

At the end of the first course, she showed me a rather sinister-looking pointed pearl embedded in a bejewelled box on the table. From its underside were wires trailing to the edge of the table. This was the bell that she used to summon the servants. If you pressed the pointed pearl which was on the top of it, it would ring, summoning the butlers or whoever was needed at the time. She said, 'Now, Colin, I call this the Borgia bell.'

I had no idea who the Borgias were, but she continued, 'The Borgias were an Italian family who lived during the Middle Ages and were famous for bumping off their guests. They would invite people that they did not like for dinner and kill them in many different ways. The Borgia bell goes back to when this family had a bell with a spike on top, which you pressed to make it ring. They would invite their guests to hit the bell to make it sound, but these guests were unaware that the tip had been spiked with poison. When they hit it, it invariably punctured their skin and killed them.'

The Queen Mother recounted this story to me in gleeful detail and then smiled and said, 'Now, Colin, would you care to press the Borgia bell and we shall have our next course.'

I gave it a good whack, and bloody hell it was painful. I thought, what if she's trying to poison me! Luckily, I survived, and throughout my two years at her side she would often ask me to ring the Borgia bell. It was her little joke. It came up regularly. Over the later months, she would invite various people to press the bell. Occasionally it would be a noisy guest. The Queen Mother might not tell them the story but instead would look at me with lips upturned as they pressed and winced. I felt as if I had been invited into a conspiracy, albeit just for fun. It was wonderful.

The meal itself was unmemorable, in so much as it was quite simple: a sort of eggs Florentine for starters – those eggy starters were a favourite of hers – followed by meat with boiled potatoes and vegetables, and chocolate fondant for pudding. What was memorable was her fondness for red wine, particularly heavy clarets which she loved. We must have gone through a bottle and a half at that first meeting. I was later to discover that she was a devoted drinker. That's not to say she was an alcoholic, far from it, it was just that she loved social drinking and of course her life was very social. She would have her first drink at noon, which would be a gin and Dubonnet – two parts Dubonnet to one part gin, a pretty potent mix. She rarely went a day without having at least one of these and getting the mix right was crucial. For official engagements, I would go ahead to the venue a few days before and instruct the waiting staff on the correct way to put the drink together. On occasion, I would have to take a bottle of Dubonnet along with me. It is not a standard drink these days.

The gin and Dubonnet would then be followed by red wine with her lunch and, very occasionally, a glass of port to end it.

Later, at the end of the day, we would approach what the Queen Mother referred to as 'the magic hour'. The magic hour was 6.00 in the evening because this was the accepted time when one could have an evening drink and the Queen Mother would sometimes say to me 'Colin, are we at the magic hour?'

I would then rather flamboyantly look at my watch, raise an eyebrow and say to her, 'Yes, ma'am, I think it's just about time,' before popping off to mix her a Martini.

Mixing a Martini was a bit of an event in itself. It consisted of gin with a sensation of vermouth. I would fill a glass with ice before pouring in the gin. Then I would squeeze lemon rind all round the edge of the glass before twisting some of the lemon juice into the gin. The vermouth would be poured into the screwcap of the bottle and the contents held over the glass (the right way up so that it didn't spill) so that some of the fumes from the vermouth would somehow miraculously waft into the gin and be absorbed into it. I would then pour the vermouth in the cap back into the bottle. After a couple of these, the Queen Mother would sit down to dinner and drink one or two glasses of pink champagne. This was always Veuve Clicquot, which she insisted on, and she would never have more than about two glasses, leaving the rest of the bottle to be collected and finished off by the staff backstairs. She stuck to this routine the whole time I was there.

I went away after my first meeting with the Queen Mother thinking, this is going to be quite a thing to get through, especially with the amount I would have to drink.

I have never really been much of a drinker and anything more than a glass or two, particularly at lunchtimes, finishes me off. And I had also never been for an interview like that before. It was very chatty, but also quite subtle. In her own very informal way the Queen Mother had found out exactly what she needed to know about me. But in return, I was certain I had blown my chance because the whole thing just seemed a bit too relaxed. All this changed when, a week later, I got a call to say that I had got the job. All I could think was, well, I can always return to flying helicopters, but this job will never come round again. And so it began.

My predecessor as equerry was a young Australian chap called Edward Dawson-Daimer, who was the son of Lord Portarlington and also an Irish Guards officer, as all the Queen Mother's equerries are. He loved all the schmoozing and meeting people and on my first day he told me, 'This is a great place to meet eligible girls. They're everywhere here at the Palace.'

Sure enough, he would organise the occasional drinks party at Clarence House where the only invitees seemed to be tall, blonde-haired and short-skirted personal assistants and secretaries from places like St James's Palace and other royal households. In they would trot and he basically got the pick of them, not bad if you were into Sloaney pony types. So for the next three months this cross between Alfie and Austin Powers acted as my guide, as I was gradually introduced into my new role which started just before the Queen Mother's birthday in August 1994.

I remember my first day quite vividly because a lunch was being held for the handover to a new commanding officer of the Black Watch, which the Queen Mother was endorsing. Whether I was still on a high at landing the job, I do not know, but what I do remember is sitting there eating, observing what was going on and drinking and drinking and drinking. I was encouraged to keep the guests company measure for measure and over the long afternoon this meant rather a lot of alcohol. I became quite the worse for wear.

At the end of October the handover took place and I was on my own.

There then followed a two-year rollercoaster ride of trips to important places of massive historical interest that, to this day, I would never have had the chance of seeing if I had not landed this dream role – I stayed at the Royal Lodge in Windsor Great Park, Sandringham, Balmoral, Birkhall, the Castle of Mey and Walmer Castle to name but a few places.

On my first day alone in the job, I was collared by a slightly stern member of the Queen Mary Knitting Guild, who said to me, 'Who are you?'

I explained that I was Equerry to the Queen Mother and she said very disparagingly: 'Well, you probably don't understand what pressure is just doing lunches here and dinner parties there. I have to arrange thousands of knitting patterns a year and co-ordinate lots of ladies all round the country. The pressure of the whole thing you probably would not be able to understand.'

I had just spent the last few years flying helicopters with

the Army, some of which was spent in Northern Ireland ferrying casualties to hospital. I remember standing there looking at her and thinking, what sort of world have I just walked into? I felt a sudden desire to get into an argument with her, but that would not have been the most auspicious of introductions to this life of duty.

Generally, life at Clarence House was very pleasant. There wasn't much running around and there were few, if any, raised voices. It was all very relaxed. I was accepted into the Queen Mother's inner circle – the treasurer, private secretary and the ladies-in-waiting – virtually straight away, which was important because this had not always been the case with previous equerries, and they ended up struggling to cope with the role and found themselves somewhat ostracised. For some barmy reason, one young chap took it upon himself to pick arguments with the Queen Mother, so that within a couple of months of being installed in the post he was told that there was an urgent need for him to return to his regiment for 'operational' reasons. He was fired, basically. But the whole point of the job was that no equerry was ever fired. If the Queen Mother found your face didn't fit, you would be told your regiment needed you to take up a posting in Northern Ireland, or somewhere like that. These days it would probably have been Iraq. It was all done by nods and winks. If you upset the Queen Mother, there was a whole number of exciting reasons for returning to your unit, or being given an RTU, as it was known. One equerry narrowly escaped an RTU after being constantly late. The penny dropped after the Queen Mother got him an alarm clock as a Christmas present!

But I made sure I was never late by getting in at 9.45 every morning to start work at 10.00. It was fifteen minutes by motorbike to Clarence House from my one-bedroom flat in Stockwell, and on arriving I would be given tea and biscuits by an orderly before consulting the desk diary to see what needed to be done. For the next hour or so, I would be on the telephone organising the Queen Mother's week and then it would be lunchtime. We would sit down to eat between 12.30 and 1.00 and this would last for a couple of hours, if I was lucky, and then there would be more phone calls to make and enquiries to follow up as a result of lunch before afternoon tea at 5.30 in the lady-in-waiting's office.

These meetings were not compulsory, but they were vital in the sense that it was the only time the inner circle of equerry, treasurer, private secretary and lady-in-waiting could get together and have the sort of conversation that they wouldn't normally have in the presence of the Queen Mother on topics such as newspaper reports and general staff gossip. If you missed these meetings, you could bet your life that the subject of the conversation would be you. It was at these get-togethers that Ralph would always ask me who I had booked in for lunch for the coming weeks and you could guarantee that if I named someone he wasn't aware of, he would reply, 'Do we know them?'

This could have been his catchphrase, but it wasn't said in a snobbish way. It was a way of making connections and a way of making introductions easier when these guests arrived at Clarence House. Ralph would always want to know a person's status or social background, so he could tell the Queen Mother in order for her to bring it up when she met them. It was a way of breaking the ice and making guests feel comfortable and at ease. It was another way of saying, can I have a background check on this person so that I can pass it on to the Queen Mother.

Following afternoon tea, I would generally fix the Queen Mother a drink before leaving. I very rarely stayed for dinner at Clarence House.

So I was learning the ropes and generally getting on well, when a few days after the handover, I almost came unstuck over the sticky problem of how one addressed other members of staff. My initial intuition was to treat the lower orders as subordinates and address them as such, much in the same way as I had learned in the Army. Thus an early encounter with one of the Queen Mother's chauffeurs had me telling him, 'Okay, the Queen Mum needs to leave at nine. Be here at eight forty-five prompt, ready to leave.'

To which he replied, 'Well, not if you ask me like that.'

I was astounded. 'What do you mean?' I spluttered. 'It's your job.'

'Well, not if you just tell me what to do it's not.'

This was absurd. How the hell was I going to get the Queen Mother from A to B if the staff were going to ignore my orders? So I gave it to him straight: 'You are the chauffeur, it's your job. Be there fifteen minutes before departure to collect the Queen Mother.'

'No!' he replied.

I walked away in despair. Twenty minutes later, I was being ticked off by the private secretary over how I had spoken to the chauffeur. Alastair said, 'Look, you can't speak like that to the chauffeur; he is a very emotional person.'

'But it's his job,' I pleaded.

'I know it's his job,' he said, 'but you just have to approach it in a very nice kind of conversational way.'

It ended up with me going back to the chauffeur with my tail between my legs and saying to him 'Well look, erm, John, the Queen Mother needs to be at this place at ten past nine. Could you possibly see your way to picking her up at, ooh, I don't know, maybe ten to nine perhaps. How does that fit in with you? Would that be okay?'

To which he responded, 'Of course I will, it'll be a pleasure!'

I walked away thinking that the whole place was utterly mad.

CHAPTER TWO

DON'T MENTION
THE WAR!

The Queen Mother was an enigma. No other woman in Europe has been so feared and so loved. During World War II, she was asked if she would remove her two young daughters from London during the Blitz. Her reply was brutal, to the point and has gone down in history; she said: 'The girls will not leave unless I do. I will not leave unless the King does. And the King will never leave.'

This act of supreme defiance caused Hitler to brand her the most dangerous woman in Europe and a year later German planes flew down the Mall and bombed Buckingham Palace while the King and Queen were there, prompting her – again famously – to comment: 'At least now I can look the people of the East End of London in the face.' It was this defiant and invulnerable streak that made you feel that if you were standing with the Queen Mother and she approved of something you did, you were bullet-proof. A typical example of this came at Clarence House during a lunch party. I would sometimes go rollerblading round the park and I was told off by a general at the party for doing this. He said to me, 'I don't think it's very appropriate for a Guards officer to be rollerblading.'

What could I say? This man was senior in rank to me so I had to respect his authority and couldn't really tell him where to go. I started spluttering a bit, not really knowing what to do, but the Queen Mother had obviously overheard the whole conversation and she came straight over and said, 'Oh, General, Colin rollerblades in the park. Don't you think that's wonderful?'

He went crimson and could hardly get his words out as he replied, 'Yes, ma'am. I think it's… tremendous.'

I could hardly believe my ears. I realised then that whatever anybody said could be completely overturned by the Queen Mother. Here was a general who, with a passing comment from her, would drop his opinion on something completely. It was a crazy situation. But not as crazy in hindsight, because all the Queen Mother was doing was protecting her inner circle. Loyalty worked both ways with her. But the bottom line was that she could say what she wanted when she wanted and no one would disagree with her. And it was this inner strength and self-confidence that I found so beguiling. She would often give me guidance on life and encourage me to be confident and open and friendly with everyone I met. When you get someone with ninety plus years of experience, as she had, giving you advice and tips you take them and act on them. One of her favourite pieces of advice, which she told me a number of times, was: 'Colin, whenever we are having a drinks or dinner party you must always greet people at the door as if they are your long lost friends and make them feel comfortable, and keep pouring the drinks until they say stop. At the end of the evening, wave them off and don't stop waving until they are out of sight.'

She gave this advice to all her staff and we all listened and followed it.

To be involved with someone so confident and seemingly bullet-proof was wonderful. I just kept thinking, here was such a caring and sincere woman and yet she had been feared by Hitler. She cared about everyone who worked for her, or who passed through her life. To her, a cleaner had just the same emotions and strength of feeling as, for example, the prime minister, and if they felt upset or aggrieved, then their point of view was just as valid as someone else's. Everyone revered her and her way of life, Prince Charles especially. He understood her outlook and stance on life completely. She just took things as they presented themselves. Hers was an old, innocent world and her approach to life was one that was dying out. I found that I fitted into this world quite easily.

Coming from an Army background I could always fall back on the tradition, etiquette and formal routine I was used to in the military. I instinctively knew what to do, and confidence in meeting people stems from knowing that you are doing the right thing. If you know how to address people, you are in good shape and everything is fine. Some people meeting the Queen Mother were reduced to nervous wrecks because they just didn't know the correct procedure or even how to address her. This is where breeding comes in. Being 'well bred' really comes down to an innate knowledge of how to be comfortable in certain social situations. Some of the people who visited Clarence House were fazed by everything around them and others were completely at ease with it all. Usually, I found that the higher a person was up the social ladder, and particularly so with high-ranking military guests, the more at ease with themselves and those around them they were. And, if an occasion needed livening up, the Queen Mother as the greatest of social operators was more than willing to step in and chivvy things along. On one occasion, when she was entertaining guests who included the Archbishop of Canterbury and various military officers, things were moving a bit slowly and the party seemed to be breaking up into cliques, so she grabbed hold of one of the generals and pushed him over to the other side of the room, saying 'Well, go on, go and talk to them then'. She then turned to me and said, 'It's just like being with children. I have to encourage them, otherwise they won't say hello.'

I thought it was just wonderful. She broke down the awkwardness of the situation and within a few minutes the party was in full swing. It was easy for the Queen Mother to break the ice at parties because people just blossomed in her presence and nobody was ever rude to her. If they were – and I believe some people had been in the past – they were given short shrift by her and you would never see them again. But everybody I encountered was quite reverential in her presence and they included staunch anti-royalists. There were times on walkabouts when one of her protection officers would tip me off about a certain person who was going to be there who could present a problem or cause some sort of commotion and I was told to be on guard and watchful. So I would prepare myself for a possible confrontation only to find that when the Queen Mother turned up they would go quiet. It really was the strangest thing. Prince Charles has a similar effect on people. I was present at one of his Highgrove dinner parties where an Australian woman friend of mine, who didn't like the idea of royalty at all, kept asking me, 'What's so special about the Royal Family? When Charles turns up, I'm not going to curtsey and later on I'm going to tell him what I really think about the Monarchy.'

Of course, when Prince Charles arrived, he exuded this natural warmth and charm, much more so than when you see him on television, and she was just blown away. She gave the deepest curtsey you have ever seen and was a model of deference and politeness. I smiled at her and she just shrugged her shoulders as if to say what can I do, the man is just too nice to be rude to. However, Prince Charles has ways of getting out of tricky situations and one of his favourite exits from awkward questions, particularly from women who try to be too forward with him, is to make light of what is said with a big smile. On one walkabout a woman approached him and said, 'You're nice, can I have kiss?'

After the briefest of awkward pauses, he immediately sprung to life with a beaming smile and laughed and said, 'Oh, you do say the funniest things,' before moving swiftly on.

I was always aware throughout my two years' service that I was working for a woman whom history would remember for a long, long time. She was born Elizabeth Angela Marguerite Bowes Lyon, the ninth of ten brothers and sisters, on 4 August 1900, while Queen Victoria was still on the throne, and she spent her early childhood at Glamis Castle in Scotland, which was originally a hunting lodge for the early kings of Scotland. The royal connection seems to run through the place like blue blood. In 1034, King Malcolm II was wounded in a battle nearby and died in the castle and a room there is named after him. Fast forward 350 years and the seeds of the present family were sown when Sir John Lyon married Princess Joanna, the widowed daughter of King Robert II, who granted the feudal barony of Glamis to his son-in-law and the family prospered, and I mean, really prospered. By the start of the seventeenth century, they were regarded as the wealthiest in Scotland, but their wealth was squandered by the 2nd Earl of Strathmore to help finance an army of Covenanters. However, it was recovered by the 3rd Earl, who became Earl of Strathmore and Kinghorne, a title that survives to this day.

In the eighteenth century, the 9th Earl married the wealthy heiress Mary Eleanor Bowes and he also became Lord Bowes, inheriting estates in England, and adopted the present name of Bowes Lyon as the family name. The then

Lady Elizabeth spent much of her early years playing with her younger brother, David, who was born twenty-one months after her. One of their favourite games involved pouring buckets of water from the battlements of Glamis onto 'invaders' below. Their relaxed attitude was probably a reflection of their parents', who, rather than being stiff and aristocratic, were very friendly and genial towards their staff. Something that I could see had rubbed off on the Queen Mother. She had more warmth and compassion towards her employees than any other member of the Royal Family.

My one regret is that we never travelled to Glamis while I was with her. It would have been wonderful to see the place, but the Queen Mother never really spoke about it, nor her brother. Her only reference to her early years was in passing when she told me: 'My mother had advised me that, when walking past a certain gentleman's club in London when I was in my late teens, I was not to look into it because it was a very bad place. She kept telling me never to look in the window. So I never did. But once when I was walking past it, a man walking towards me suddenly stopped and said, "Oh, blue eyes." He had no idea who I was.'

This really thrilled her because I think it was the first time her looks had been commented on and, although she must only have been about nineteen, she was becoming aware that men were seeing her no longer as a young girl but as an attractive woman. But it was rare for her to bring up the subject of her family like this. Her family was never really a topic of conversation in my presence; it was just another part of her life that had passed along with most of her friends.

She was not one for dwelling on what had gone, although she did like to talk about World War II.

Secret documents only recently released show that when Britain faced its darkest hour, during the Dunkirk evacuation, plans were drawn up in the case of any German invasion to spirit away Princesses Elizabeth and Margaret to the home of the Earl and Countess Beauchamp, Madresfield Court, just outside Malvern, where they would stay until King George VI and the Queen could join them from Buckingham Palace. A month later, the government drew up plans to evacuate the princesses to Canada. But Queen Elizabeth famously said no and they stayed. By 1941, when fear of German invasion was at its height, five officers and 124 troops of the Coldstream Guards had been set aside to evacuate the Royal Family. Using ten armoured vehicles they were to move them between seven remote country houses, depending on how successful Britain was in beating off German invaders, before ultimately taking them out of the country if it looked like the Nazis would be successful. I often remember the Queen Mother saying to other guests and myself: 'The King had no intention of abandoning Britain. We would have seen it out to the bitter end. You do not abandon your country.'

She was ninety-four years old when I started the job and ninety-six when I left and she coped with old age brilliantly, being much sprightlier than people half her age. Add to this the fact that she was completely alert and you had quite a formidable old lady, though she did nearly come a cropper and kill herself in my presence during a walk in the grounds of the Castle of Mey, when she slipped on a mossy step and almost went tumbling down a flight of concrete stairs. As she fell backwards, I managed to grab her by the lapels of her coat and hoist her back onto her feet. The funny thing was that after saving her life in such a dramatic way, she didn't say thank you and I didn't ask her if she was all right. Etiquette prevented such an exchange. In her eyes, I was doing my job in preventing her from falling and, for my part, to ask her if she was okay would have almost been an admission that she had made a mistake. How bizarre is that? So we just carried on walking and it was never mentioned again.

This business of doing the right thing was the way she had lived all her life; it was a world in which you never let your true feelings show and always maintained an air of calm and placid detachment. The Queen Mother never got annoyed or angry with anyone or anything during the whole time I was with her and she took a detached view of virtually everything. If something did upset her, she would say 'Oh, isn't that annoying?' But there was no emotion involved and throughout her life she never really talked about any personal loss or her private feelings – people of her generation rarely did. Similarly, she never expressed a personal opinion on anything, at least not one that could be considered controversial, not that she didn't have controversial opinions. Early in her marriage to the then Duke of York, she had been severely told off by George V for giving an interview to the press and this hit her for six and she never let her true feelings be shown in front of anyone other than her family ever again.

The media became a tool for her to peddle the notion of the Royal Family doing the right thing for the nation, and everything to do with television and newspapers that involved her was very considered. She would never give an interview or go on television unless it was absolutely necessary and that is why she was hardly ever seen in the media apart from on special occasions such as her birthday. So newspaper reports came down to little nuggets that reporters could pick up from friendly members of staff. As a result, her actions have often been reported and repeated time and again on television and in the newspapers, such as when she came across a group of teenagers throwing stones at cars and, winding down the window of her passing Daimler, asked them, 'Whatever would American tourists think?' Another excellent quote that was widely reported was her comment, 'Is it just me or are pensioners getting younger these days?'

The Queen is similar: she never expresses her views in public. The closest she ever came to expressing in public how she truly felt was in describing her *annus horribilis*, her bad year of 1992, which people still refer to even today. But personal loss, grief, turmoil and emotion had been at the centre of the Queen Mother's life for well over half a century; there was the abdication of King Edward VIII, the Second World War and the loss of her husband King George VI in 1952, to mention but a few examples. I think one of the saddest aspects about her life was that by the end of my time working for her, the Queen Mother had lost about ninety-five per cent of the friends she had known, simply because she had outlived them all, and this tempered her views on death. When your first real friend dies, it is shocking and you grieve, but by the time your umpteenth friend has passed away you have become more used to it, and this is what had happened with the Queen Mother. I remember when we were staying at Sandringham in 1995 and Ralph went to see his best friend who was seriously ill and close to death. By the time he got there he only had a few hours with his old pal before the poor fellow died. On returning to Sandringham, the Queen Mother asked him, 'Oh, how was your friend?'

To which an ashen-faced Ralph replied, 'Well, he died, ma'am.'

She looked at him and just said, 'Oh well.'

And that was that. But it wasn't said in a glib way. It was recognition of the fact that there is little one can say in a situation like that, and her way of saying that one element of life is death and you just have to get on with things.

Ralph responded with a simple 'Ah, yes' and got back to his work.

This stoicism had become entrenched in her psyche and there was no way anybody would ever change it. It was the same stoic determination that had got her through World War II. She lived in a world of formality, where she would never have involved herself in a drunken knees-up, or put her arm around someone as a way of comforting them. Everything in her life had a set format and the rules were there and they served a purpose. The purpose of the routine at Clarence House was to make her life as comfortable as possible. But despite living this rigorous, antiquated life, she did have a mischievous streak and loved to turn situations on their head. One of her favourite ruses was to sneak out of Clarence House whenever David Linley, her grandson, paid her a visit to go for a spin in his sports car. She loved the fact that she was being smuggled away without her protection officers seeing her, and she got a buzz out of doing things she wasn't supposed to do. She did like being a bit naughty. I remember one evening at Birkhall when there were no guests and it was just her and the home team and she said to me, 'Colin, let's ring round and see if someone wants to come in for a drink.'

'Certainly, ma'am,' I said.

I was about to pick up the phone to invite someone from one of the Scottish regiments when she added, 'Let's invite the minister and his wife for a game of cards. We could play poker!' and she smiled at me.

For a second my heart raced. I thought, how the hell can I phone a Scottish clergyman and ask him to come over to Birkhall for a gambling session? He would have me damned for all eternity. But then I realised she was joking and smiled back, more out of relief than anything else.

That mischievous streak in her also manifested itself during official visits to factories and civic buildings and the like. She would be following an itinerary that had been strictly set when suddenly she would see a closed door that her party wasn't really supposed to go through and she would ask, 'Oh, what's this room for?'

She refused to be railroaded on these sorts of trips. If

anyone was going to do the railroading, it was going to be her. At airports, if she was waiting to fly somewhere, she might see one of the aeroplane staff refuelling a plane or a cleaner on his or her rounds and would ask to speak to them. There then ensued a lengthy conversation, far longer than she would have had with any high-ranking airport boss who was officially supposed to meet her. She had become quite bored, after nearly 100 years, of being presented with people whom her organisers thought she should meet. This is also one of Prince Charles's big gripes. He only really gets to meet people chosen by his members of staff and he does find it intensely irritating. Most members of the Royal Family will try and grab someone who isn't part of the agenda because when they are trapped in a bubble it is quite nice for them to break out once in a while, albeit for just a few minutes. The one thing the Queen Mother didn't like about itineraries and agendas was the whole idea of the media scrum – the jostling that represented the press photographers desperate for the picture, which would sell newspapers and make them a tidy sum. She disliked the thought of organised photo calls where she would be expected to pose for a picture and would use all her wiliness and guile to overcome the problem. At a Field of Remembrance service at which I was present, there was a huge press pack waiting with cameras ready as she signed the visitors' book. But unlike at celebrity functions, they showed slightly more respect for the Queen Mother than they would for other Royals and didn't ask her outright for a photograph. She didn't want to do a staged one either, so she looked up into each and every camera lens in a broad sweeping turn of her head and said, with a big smile on her face, 'Has anybody got the time?' All you could hear was click, click, click and more clicks.

Her treatment by the press was immense and totally different to the sort of press her grandchildren got. None of the press ever hounded her, and everyone played by her rules and was utterly charming to her. So she played and handled the press in a totally differently way than, say, Charles and Diana did. They tried to use the press as a weapon to hurt each other and other people. Because of this they were seen as fair game by newspapers such as the *Sun*, the *Mail* and the *Mirror* who tore into them like savages. The Queen Mother never used the press in this way and would never make a destructive point through the medium of a newspaper. She really wasn't interested in doing anything negative like that and, as a result, she was respected much more in those sorts of circles than Charles and Diana and all her grandchildren, if the truth be told. By the time she was in her nineties, her involvement with television and newspapers simply involved making sure she was available for photos if the event demanded. Whenever anything negative came out about the Royal Family, it left her deeply disappointed. I remember saying to her, 'Did you see the Dimbleby interview with Prince Charles on TV?'

The look she gave me could have frozen fire. There was a smile there but she spoke through gritted teeth and her eyes narrowed slightly as she said, 'Some things are best not discussed.' She meant that he shouldn't have done it and, probably more pointedly, I shouldn't be asking her about it.

She firmly believed that all her family should never go on record about anything that was even slightly contentious and they should keep their views to themselves. But it was hard for her to ignore all the negative press that was flying around. If she read a report that she deemed insulting to her family, she would mutter, 'Oh gosh, not this again.'

The years when I was at Clarence House proved to be quite a hard time for her because she was very old-fashioned and an extremely private person. With stories such as 'Camillagate' breaking and all the talk of tampons and such like, one can imagine how awkward that would be for anyone to read, let alone the Queen Mother who was utterly embarrassed and refused to talk about these things to anyone, even her closest friends. If anyone did bring up the subject of Charles and Diana's marriage, they would be quickly diverted to something else, mainly by the Queen Mother saying, 'Have some more wine and tell me about…'. This was a woman who disapproved if someone went out incorrectly dressed. To go out into the world and reveal the most intimate problems in a relationship was really not on in her mind.

The majority of media enquiries were handled by Alastair on behalf of the Queen Mother and he did most of the press releases. But by that time there was no great demand for the Queen Mother because everyone knew she didn't make her opinions known in public, so it was a bit of a fruitless task to ring up anyway. The majority of calls we took were from people like Jennie Bond, who was the BBC's royal correspondent before the call of the jungle in *I'm A Celebrity, Get Me Out Of Here!* took her on to new ventures.

I spoke to Jennie quite a lot on the phone. She seemed busy to the point of manic. One minute she was in this country, the next thousands of miles away. She frequently asked to come in and look at something or other or to get some background material from us. She was a typical television royal correspondent. I did find that the more discreet they were, as was Jennie, the better they seemed to do their job. As soon as they started to become a little bit aggressive and tried to dish the dirt, everybody simply closed ranks and wouldn't talk to them. It was quite an odd relationship with the press that I would describe as love–hate. Jennie was good because she was so professional. She didn't try to inflame things and she didn't ask pointed questions, so people didn't mind talking to her, plus she was very mindful of protocol and that is the strength of a good royal correspondent. There were other reporters, mainly from the tabloids, who were constantly after the inside scoop, obviously because of the nature of the newspaper they worked for. But most people who were close to royalty and had the inside knowledge that these journalists were after didn't like that kind of approach. The successful ones were the ones who respected the system, dressed appropriately and observed protocol when in front of senior members of the Royal Family. But, on the other hand, you always got certain junior employees who were willing to sell stories to the press behind their employers' backs and I strongly suspect this was going on at Clarence House. I would often spot a story in a newspaper about the Queen Mother and wonder where it came from because it certainly didn't come from her. Fortunately, most of the stories weren't negative anyway, but I suspect that most of the junior butlers and some of the cooks were on the payroll of at least one Fleet Street newspaper. They were not on great salaries so this was an easy way of boosting their income, plus they were easy to infiltrate.

None of the home team ever sold anything to the press; we just tolerated the fact that this went on, though in the years I was there, I don't think I can recall any bad press for the Queen Mother. If she had her royal correspondents of choice, they would have been the Dimblebys, and this extended to nearly all the senior members of the Royal Family. I remember asking Ralph why the Royals were so keen on this family and he said, 'It's because of their background. The Royal Family feel much more comfortable in the presence of people from a similar background to theirs. It's all down to breeding. They wouldn't really like disclosing family secrets to someone from a comprehensive school.'

The Queen Mother did have her paper of choice, it was the *Daily Telegraph*, but she read the newspapers less and less as the scandal stories broke on an almost daily basis throughout the mid nineties. If she passed a newspaper and caught the headline, be it about Charles and Diana or Andrew and Fergie, she would utter words of disappointment and go quiet for a bit and become slightly withdrawn. Everything that was going on exasperated her. She couldn't understand why they behaved as they did. In the fifties and sixties the newspapers had left the Royal Family in peace but it all changed for the worse in the eighties and nineties. The Queen Mother couldn't understand the new tabloid culture that had arisen around the birth of the *Sun* newspaper, and the whole concept of modernising the Monarchy and dragging it from the past into the present – which effectively began when the Royals threw open the doors of the Palace for a television documentary in the late sixties – seemed completely alien to her. In her eyes, the whole idea of modernisation and embracing the media just seemed to entail more bad publicity for her grandchildren, and ideas being bandied about at the time regarding the Royal Family's having to pay taxes and certain lesser Royals being struck off the Civil List were kept well away from her ears. It would have completely undermined her life and upset her. She and her daughters had a duty to serve the State as ambassadors of the nation. For the State to repay this devotion to duty by making her family pay taxes would have been too hideous for her to bear.

She had no concept of modernising anything. There wasn't even a computer in Clarence House and right up until her death everything was done by hand. She liked things the way they were and, as a woman in her mid nineties, there was absolutely no way she was ever going to change her lifestyle. The world at Clarence House quite rightly revolved around her and that was that, and in this sense she didn't always keep up with changing trends and the biggest at that time was the concept of political correctness.

She was quite fond of being un-PC and didn't like the notion of political correctness, thinking it nonsense. She would say things to me such as: 'It's not politically correct to look down on our European neighbours, is it? But I still find the Germans beastly.'

It was the same with food fads and diets. She had never gone on a diet in her life and was never going to, but it didn't stop her from saying to me, 'People say it's not good to eat butter. People say butter is bad for your heart. Well, I have eaten butter all my life and look at me.'

How could you argue with a woman of ninety-four saying that? And she did love butter. She slapped it on to her toast and bread with gusto, great lumps of it.

She also had a thing about the class system and was what I would term a reluctant aristocrat. There was nothing pompous or pretentious about her whatsoever; she didn't need to be. People are pompous when they feel socially threatened or believe that they are above someone in terms of their job or social standing. But the Queen Mother was at the pinnacle of the social stratum. There really was no need on her account to be aggressive or pompous because she didn't have to prove anything. She liked to poke fun at the whole social categorisation frenzy that was still at large in class-ridden Britain. One of her favourite comments to me was when she would hold up a piece of bread and say, 'Colin, aristocrats call these rolls. Everyone else calls them buns. What do you call them? I call them buns because I'm not an aristocrat.'

The Royals are in a class of their own. Historically, they

were and always have been served by the upper classes, which put them above this bracket in many respects. Describing the Royal Family as upper class would be like drawing a parallel between the role of an astronaut and an airline pilot. They both fly, but there is such a difference. The Royal Family is in a completely different world and the members of it live their life in their own little bubble that is far removed from anything you would ever find outside the palace gates. But I found myself under more pressure in terms of social graces and manners at things like Army dinners than when with the Royal Family – which made me realise that the further away you get from the centre of royalty the more rigid formality becomes, whereas if I were having lunch with the Queen Mother and wanted to use a different fork, or even my hands where appropriate, to eat my food, she would make everything alright. At one lunch, a guest picked up his soup bowl and drank straight from it. Quick as a flash the Queen Mother said, 'I always think soup tastes much better that way.'

If anyone had considered looking on disapprovingly, they certainly didn't after that. And that was the wonderful thing about the Queen Mother. She could rewrite the rules as she went along. With her you just had to behave in a decent and civilised manner at all times.

Leisure time, or what I would class as time she spent alone, was limited and therefore very precious to her. She spent a lot of it napping, usually because she had been through a heavy lunch or dinner, or on a shooting and fishing trip, or a visit, but when she didn't sleep she would watch television. Her favourite programme by a mile was *Fawlty Towers*. I'm not joking when I say she must have watched it over thirty times in the two years I was there and she always found it funny. Her favourite bit was the one with the Germans and the whole 'Don't mention the war' thing. She would often quote from *Fawlty Towers* if the moment asked for it. If a lunch guest asked her if she had enjoyed her food, she would reply, '"It's delicious and nutritious."'

A couple of times we had veal for lunch and on both occasions she turned to me and asked, 'What do you think of the meal, Colin? I think it's veally good.'

She chose her moments and really came out with some funny things. She was always saying 'Don't mention the war', but never when she had Germans present, funnily enough. She also paraphrased another moment involving the character of the Major and would say to me, 'Do you know the thing about German women, Colin? Good card players.' And she would point in a perfect mimic of the Major then laugh heartily and say, 'Oh I do love that show.'

Another favourite programme of hers was *Keeping Up Appearances*; she found Hyacinth Bucket and her over-the-top affectations extremely funny. When she wasn't watching comedy, she would generally watch horse racing if she watched anything. Very occasionally, she would see a film that David Linley brought in for her. He would just rent whatever was out at the time. It could be anything from *Four Weddings and a Funeral* to *Jurassic Park*. But she wasn't that keen on watching movies that went on for more than a couple of hours because she found that she started to fall asleep midway through them. Occasionally, she would say, 'I understand there's a good documentary on about this or that, could you get hold of it for me?'

So I would either tape it or, if it were available in the video shop, I would rent it out.

Her favourite documentaries were about the wars, be it the Great War or the Second World War. When I left Clarence House after two years and went into television, I did a series on World War II and the rise of the Nazi party. It was a potted history of the party up to the outbreak of hostilities. I gave her a box set and she really loved it and every time I went back after that – former equerries were invited to lunch once every couple of months after they left – it was virtually all she talked about for the whole meal.

Her other main interest was music. She especially loved Scottish piped music and easy listening, such as Frank Sinatra, Perry Como and Dean Martin. But for some bizarre reason she also enjoyed yodelling songs. She thought they were so bad they were actually good and she had this huge fascination for them. In effect they were so corny and so bloody awful that at times I just wanted to break the records into tiny little pieces and have done with them. But her big thrill, fortunately, was singers like Bing Crosby, Fred Astaire and the easy-listening melodies of people like Carol Gibbons; she was a big fan of Carol Gibbons. Had she ever have appeared on *Desert Island Discs*, I am sure Carol Gibbons would have been her record of choice to take with her to this desert island. Her favourite songs were things like 'Riptide', which I heard on at least a dozen occasions.

Strangely enough, she wasn't that bothered by opera music, although she did like some classical music, mainly Mozart, but not as much as her easy-listening collection. She would listen to music in the early evening when I was mixing her a Martini. But she didn't choose the records herself; more often than not, it was left to me to stick something on the record player, especially if we had guests. If it were just the home team there, everybody just chipped in, making their own drinks and choosing records on behalf of the Queen Mother. Sometimes I would say to her, 'How about a bit of yodelling, ma'am?'

She would laugh and reply, 'Oh, marvellous.'

But she did like people making their own decisions about what music to play, as long as it was from her collection.

She also had a passion for military music which she didn't really have on tape but would listen to at big events. The music composed for her 100th birthday is the one thing that sticks in my mind. It is utterly, utterly moving. The bagpipes, or agony pipes as I like to call them, were another big love of hers. But things like pop music had completely passed her by. Her musical tastes were stuck somewhere in the fifties and sixties and didn't extend too much into the nineties, if at all. And her Scottish ancestry had given her a love of reeling, or cross-country dancing as I call it. She loved it, absolutely loved it. At Birkhall, we had evenings of Scottish dancing and the Queen Mother loved people taking part and would sit there smiling, clapping and whooping to the music and generally having a really good time. She liked her guests to have a good time as well, which is why she insisted everybody join in the dancing, and I mean everybody, including me. I was all right at it, but midway through a dance I would be wishing for it to end. I know some guests who were dragged almost kicking and screaming to their feet to perform this ritual and by the look on their face – a combination of a self-conscious smile and beetroot-red cheeks – it was obvious to me that they would rather have been dragged naked across a field of broken glass than do what they were doing, but they did it anyway. I would compare it to having to do drill practice at 5.00 in the morning in the middle of winter. But the Queen Mother loved a good dance, and so did Prince Charles. There were a couple of occasions when he joined her at Birkhall for one of these Scottish knees-up. He was a really good dancer and did genuinely enjoy himself.

As for other interests, well, things like current affairs and the state of the world had left her behind. She didn't really bother with it anymore. If anything newsworthy broke, we would inform her of it – at that time it was mainly the conflicts in the Balkans. But she was nearly 100 years old and wasn't really very bothered about what was going on in those places. She had lived through two world wars and the death of her husband. All she was interested in now was a quiet life surrounded by friends. Very occasionally, she would read a book. She enjoyed fiction and her favourite novelist was Dick Francis. Because of the racing connection she loved having him round for lunch to talk horses. But she didn't read that many books when I was there. Her eyesight was not that great and she had great difficulty reading small print. She had a magnifying glass, but found it all a bit of a strain.

Despite this, there was no slowness about her and she was never forgetful; in fact, I found her great company. Whereas most world leaders would be lucky to get ten minutes alone in her presence, I would be alone with her for at least half an hour every day, especially on picnic lunches in Scotland when we would often be alone waiting for the other guests to turn up. These moments were quite magical. She would tell me about dancing with Fred Astaire and with a glint in her eye add, 'He was quite a good dancer, you know.'

A great story she told me during those moments alone was when, during the War, she and the King went on a tour of bombed houses and shops in London's East End. She said, 'On this particular day, I had managed to get hold of a banana and I had this banana in my bag. Now, at that time, bananas hadn't really been introduced into Britain as a fruit, so many people didn't know anything about them. I remember this little girl, whose house had been bombed, came up to greet me and I gave her this banana. She said to me, "What is this? What do I do with this?"

'I said, it is a banana and you eat it. She turned to her mother who was standing right behind her and said, "Must I?"

'And her mother said, "Just eat it."

'Colin, I'm not even certain that she peeled it before taking a bite,' she said as she smiled at me.

It was a lovely moment for me; to be getting first-hand accounts of history from someone with such historic significance herself was like touring the National Gallery in the presence of van Gogh. It seemed beyond the realm of what is ordinarily possible.

CHAPTER THREE

SHOOTING SQUIRRELS
WITH A SNIPER RIFLE

'So then, what are we having for lunch today?' It was a question I often asked the staff at Clarence House shortly after I arrived for work.

'I'm not sure,' was the reply from one of the servants. 'The chef's gone on strike.'

'What! What! How am I going to break that to the Queen Mother? What the hell are we going to do? More to the point, why has he gone on strike?'

'Someone upset him,' was the reply.

'Someone upset him, someone upset him, oh my God!' I exclaimed.

This was looking bad. But it was up to me to tell her, and I did: 'Erm, ma'am, I have some bad news. The, erm, chef appears to have downed tools.'

'You mean, he's gone on strike,' she replied.

'Erm, yes, ma'am, apparently someone upset him.'

'Oh well, he's obviously a bit upset, but I'm sure he'll come round eventually and get back to work. In the meantime, we shall have to eat salads,' she said.

Sure enough, for the next few days, we ate nothing but salads, until the chef decided to come back and when he did nothing more was ever said on the matter. But it did lead me to think that judging by her response it wasn't the first time he had gone on strike, and it probably wouldn't be the last.

This was one of the most worrying moments for me because everything in the Queen Mother's life revolved around lunch. It was the most integral part of her day and they were a big, big deal; whether they were formal lunches at Clarence House, picnic lunches at Birkhall or shooting lunches at the Castle of Mey, the Queen Mother geared her whole day around lunch. She loved entertaining guests and being entertained and lunch was the nucleus of this. The main challenge for me was getting through the whole thing in a fairly sober state. It would start between 12.00 and 12.30 and on a typical day my office would be filled with about eight people; half of them staying for the meal, the other half invited just for drinks, but not to meet the Queen Mother. The half invited for drinks were generally friends of mine, or the treasurer's, the private secretary's or the lady-in-waiting's, and it was funny to see their reactions in being welcomed into this most exclusive of drinking clubs. I was a bit pathetic at these sorts of things and drank tonic water, pretending it had gin in it. But in my defence I knew what was coming later, and that was drinks with the Queen Mother which could be quite demanding.

'I don't think I will today, ma'am. I think I'll stick to water,' I would reply.

She would give me a look of mild concern and said, 'But you must have some wine.'

I told her, 'Ma'am, I can't, I must do some work this afternoon. I have a busy schedule to get through.'

But this didn't dissuade her: 'You must have some wine. How can you not have wine with your meal?'

I was telling her that I had to ring someone and meet this person and that, but she cut me short. 'Listen, Colin,' she said, her voice quietly insistent, 'Don't bother about all that. I'm sure they'll understand if you can't meet them or ring them. Now have some wine.'

And that was that, I had a glass of wine. The next thing I knew, she was saying 'Oh, Colin, have another'.

'I really can't, ma'am,' I said.

'Oh, have another, go on, you must have another.'

The trouble was she could be so persuasive – you felt that if you tried to say no, she would be deeply offended – and people just didn't say no to her anyway; it just wasn't the done thing.

So I said, 'Okay,' with a look of complete resignation on my face.

Then I would be poured a third glass of wine and all the time she would be saying, 'There you go, Colin, there's another glass' or, 'Have a top up Colin'.

On the third glass, I told her, 'I have to drive this afternoon. I've got to drive home.'

But this didn't stop her and she said, 'What's the problem with that?'

'Well, I might get stopped by the police and breathalysed.'

'Oh, just tell them you work for me,' she said, almost conspiratorially, with a big smile.

To her, that was the 'get out of jail free' card. One evening I found myself putting it to the test. I was racing back to my rented house in Bayswater with a bad headache, weaving in and out of traffic; and I was spotted by an unmarked police car that followed me and finally stopped me. The traffic policeman said, 'Do you know why I stopped you?'

I told him I could think of at least three reasons and gingerly handed him my Palace ID card when he asked for identification. He went back to the car for about three minutes, came back and simply said, 'Right, okay. Well, on your way then, but don't let this happen again.'

It did make me wonder and still does today.

But as far as driving while way over the limit, I wasn't so sure I actually would get away with it. Even so, the Queen Mother's powers of persuasion were legendary. I remember a dinner at Birkhall when I had eaten a fairly sizeable steak and felt quite full. The Queen Mother, sitting next to me, wasn't that keen on steak. It wasn't that she didn't like it, she just found it a bit too chewy, and that evening she had a simple solution to the problem: she just picked up the whole thing with her fork and deftly flicked it onto my plate and said, 'There you go, you're a growing lad, you can eat that.'

I just thought, oh my God – I was full to bursting. But I couldn't leave it, so I ate it and then had pudding, which was a particularly heavy bread-and-butter pudding. By the end of the meal, if the waiter had come round with wafer thin mints, I probably would have exploded like Mr Creosote from Monty Python's *The Meaning of Life*. Food, like drink, was another hazard of the job. The starters and main courses were not particularly fattening, but dessert was a different matter. The chefs would make it their personal challenge to come up with amazing cakes, pastries, and jam sponges, and I, as the youngest person present at these almost Tudoresque feasts, was expected to have a bit of everything. As a result, I went jogging about three or four times a week, desperate to burn off some calories. But even this could have its pitfalls.

One summer's evening I was running round the grounds of the Castle of Mey in my shorts, trainers and a T-shirt, not the sort of attire you would ever want the Queen Mother to see you in, and I remember coming in round the back of the castle and talking to Reg the butler who suddenly, as I'm chatting to him, starts staring wide-eyed over my shoulder. The next things I see are corgis round my feet and I hear a small voice behind me say, 'Colin, you're looking very appropriately dressed for a warm summer's evening'.

Christ, I thought, it's the Queen Mother, and she added, 'Could you take the dogs for a run?'

'Well, I'll try,' I replied.

So I went back out with the dogs but they were just not interested in going for any sort of run at all. The whole concept of running was totally alien to them. At one stage,

I threw a stick for them to chase and they looked at me as if to say, well, when are you going to get it then? Eventually, I settled for taking them for a very long, extended walk around the grounds and when I got back I pushed them all into the Queen Mother's drawing room where they flopped out while she slept in her chair. Then I went upstairs to shower and change into my evening clothes in time to meet guests who had arrived for pre-dinner drinks. As I was mixing with the assembled crowd, chatting to them and just generally entertaining, the Queen Mother came in. The guests bowed and nodded as she passed them, but she made a bee-line straight for me and said quite sternly, 'Colin, Colin, what did you do with the dogs, they're so exhausted?'

This room of thirty or so people, which included various senior guests and MPs, suddenly went deathly quiet. Desperately trying to think on my feet while feeling quite worried inside, I said, 'Ma'am, I tied them to the bumper of a car and took them for a drive.'

There were hushes of shock before an eerie silence descended on the room as people contemplated beheadings and the like, but the Queen Mother suddenly dropped all pretence of being annoyed, put her hand on my arm, chuckled and said, 'Oh, Colin, you are wicked!'

The room nearly collapsed with relief. I nearly collapsed full stop.

I realised after about three months of these calorific lunches that the idea of getting through them in either a fairly sober state or in one which didn't involve rapid weight gain was almost impossible. If I had had a lot to drink and felt groggy I would go back to my office, sit at my desk and pull my two desk drawers out either side so I could rest my arms in them to get my head in the right position for a nap. I would be woken up at 5.30 with tea and biscuits delivered to my desk.

By far the biggest of what I would term these eating ordeals was on a Sunday when the royal party was up in Scotland. Sundays were a day off from hunting and fishing, so, for example, a typical day at Birkhall involved rising at about 8.00 in the morning and going down to breakfast between 8.30 and 9.00. You could have whatever you wanted to eat. There was toast and jam or marmalade, cereals, porridge and fruit. It was like a buffet all spread out on a table. If you really wanted to go for it, you could have full *à la carte* which was cereal, toast, fruit juice, coffee and a full English breakfast. Now you tell me anyone who can summon the willpower to resist all that? I certainly couldn't. So, loaded with breakfast, I and the rest of the party would go to church at about 10.00. Afterwards, we had drinks and nibbles with the minister until about noon by which time we would head off back to Birkhall for pre-lunch drinks with guests who had been invited up for the day, or even the weekend, before sitting down for lunch. Lunch on a Sunday was almost invariably some egg starter followed by crayfish and asparagus. This was the Queen Mother's favourite main course, and the whole thing would go on until about 3.00 in the afternoon. An hour later, I would get in a Land Rover loaded with a hamper of scones, cakes, biscuits and the like, driving off to an estate cottage for afternoon tea. At 6.30 in the evening, we would come back to Birkhall to have pre-dinner drinks with guests before sitting down for dinner at 7.00, which again was a full three-course meal! You could never go two hours without some kind of meal being presented to you.

On the other hand, the best lunches were at Clarence House in the Green Room, which was the Queen Mother's name for eating outside in the garden beneath a huge weeping willow tree surrounded by greenery. If it were a hot day, she would say to her servants, 'I think we'll have lunch in the Green Room today.'

There was something about eating outdoors at Clarence House that made it more informal than eating indoors. But the one thing that bothered her was the squirrels, particularly the grey ones. I remember one outdoor lunch with the Queen Mother and the rest of the home team. I was watching the squirrels when she suddenly said, 'Colin, do you think you could bring a .22 rifle in one day this week and we could pick the squirrels off between courses?'

I thought she was joking, but when I turned to speak to her, I realised by the look on her face that it was a genuine question. 'Well, I, erm, I, I suppose I could,' I stammered.

'Oh good,' she said, 'Because they are a nuisance.'

After lunch, just as I was leaving, the private secretary took me to one side and said, 'Please don't bring a .22 rifle in. I think it would cause problems with the neighbours. Not to mention the police.'

Too damn right it would, I thought. But sure enough the

next day, as we were having lunch outside, the Queen Mother said, 'Did you bring the rifle in, Colin?'

'I'm afraid I didn't, ma'am. I thought it might upset the police a little.'

And with that she shrugged her shoulders and said, 'Ah well…'

Her home team joined her for all the lunches, but at least three times a week we would be joined by guests. She saw these invitations almost as a gift that she could give to people. She realised that if someone was invited to lunch at Clarence House, it really meant a great deal to them and they loved the whole experience when they came. However, they weren't really invitations at all because people were bidden to eat with her meaning they didn't really have a chance to turn her down. Guests could be split into two camps: the super polite, which consisted mainly of MPs and high-ranking military officials, and the completely strange, which tended to encompass artists and creative types.

One of the most eccentric was an Irish artist called Derek Hill, who was also a regular guest of the Prince of Wales. The Queen Mother had acquired a lot of his pictures and when he came to Clarence House she made sure that they were put out on display for him to see. So Derek would come in, look at them, spit on the sleeve of his old tweed jacket and start rubbing them, saying, 'This one could do with a bit of a clean.'

Here was a true eccentric in full flow and the wonderful thing was that this was just how the Queen Mother expected him to be. And he didn't disappoint.

While he was cleaning them, or if he turned away from her, she would look at me or one of her team and raise her eyes to Heaven before looking back and saying, 'Ah, it is a bit dusty, yes, I'll get one of the staff to look at it.'

One guest whom I particularly dreaded was Lord Slim. He was a very tall fellow, ex-Special Forces, and when you went up to greet him formally he would reply by way of a sharp punch to the stomach. The first time this happened, I practically doubled up in pain and he shouted at the top of his voice, 'Hello, young man, and how are you?'

He reminded me very much of Stephen Fry's character in *Blackadder Goes Forth*. Every time I met him, he did this. The Queen Mother would see me doubled up, smile and say, 'Oh, I see you've met Lord Slim.'

By far the guests for whom the Queen Mother reserved her biggest affection were the Special Forces. She revelled in her role as President of the Special Forces Club. One regular guest was Brian Stonehouse, an amazing person. He was an SOE – a Special Operations Executive – during the war, but got captured in 1941 near Lyons in France. The Nazis put him in solitary confinement and he was subjected to frequent and brutal interrogations before being passed from prison to prison, until he eventually ended up at the Natzweiler-Struthof concentration camp in Alsace. He managed to avoid being executed because of one thing: he was a terrific artist. Brian managed to keep himself alive by painting and doing drawings and sketches for the camp commandant. The commandant liked his art so much that he let him draw in return for keeping his life, but he didn't like him that much because he would always tell Brian his execution date was imminent. Every single week, Brian would be told that his execution had been set for the following week and he was to be hung, shot or gassed. When the day came, they would say it had been put back until the following Tuesday and that he was going to be shot. When that passed, they would tell him he was going to be gassed. They kept it up for a year and he was put under tremendous psychological pressure, but he never cracked. He was eventually sent to Dachau from where he was liberated by American troops in April 1945.

During my two years as equerry, he lived in a flat in Bayswater. He had managed to save and retrieve most of his prison camp sketches and then, tragically, his flat got broken into and they were all stolen. This would have broken a lesser man. But Brian knew the exact dimensions of all forty-odd pictures that he had drawn and he began the long, laborious process of redrawing them from memory. He was still redrawing them when I worked there. I remember going for lunches with him at the Special Forces Club in London and on the wall was a sketch of four women he had drawn. These were SOE agents who had been sent to Natzweiler-Struthof and executed by lethal injection before their remains were incinerated in the crematorium. Brian was able to testify at the war crimes trials to the women's fate. He died in 1998, aged eighty.

There were also guests of the non-human variety. Every time the Irish Guards had a new mascot, which was a wolfhound, they would bring it to Clarence House to show the Queen Mother. They brought in a new one while I was there. It was massive. If it stood on its hind legs it was about six feet four inches tall, absolutely huge. It was only a puppy as well and when it came in to meet the Queen Mother, it bounded up to her, jumped up and put its paws both side of her shoulders, looking her straight in the eyes. It was an amazing sight, but I found myself thinking, for God's sake, please don't lick or bite her. I managed to take a photograph of it and this dog is just basically staring at her. When other members of staff rushed to get it off, she just said, 'Oh, no, no, no, it's fine, it's really fine.'

Others who came for lunch were quite simply mad. I remember one guest in particular at a lunch for a group of scientific types. They were there to receive some award. One of them came up to me and said, 'I have a cure for AIDS. The remedy is locked up in a safe and I'm just waiting for the correct moment to release it.'

I thought, is it me, or is this bloke absolutely barking mad? I just said to him, 'Oh right, good, how, erm, very interesting,' and tried to get away as fast as possible.

The one quirk of having guests for lunch or dinner was that, if there were eight people or more invited, it meant following a process called directional talking, which is a rather old-fashioned way of behaving at table. Normally, you might make conversation with the people around you in a fairly arbitrary fashion; you may talk to the person on your left one minute and the next you are talking to someone across the table before going back to the person on your right. With directional talking, you are required to talk to the people sitting immediately to your left and right. Usually, the senior person there, whether it was the Queen or the Queen Mother, would start talking to the person on her immediate left. Every other person would note that and also talk to the person on their left, and that would happen for the first half of the meal. At some point, the host or hostess would pause and begin talking to the person on his or her right. And every other person around the table had to do the same. You might get the amusing situation where halfway through a conversation someone would say, 'Oh, looks like we're turning now.'

It sounds contrived, but it's actually great fun and it guarantees that you talk equally to the people on your right and left and nobody gets left out. A lot of dinner parties are free-for-alls where you don't get to talk to somebody for a great length of time. But with this you cannot escape it.

I quickly worked out that when the Queen Mother was in London, lunches were the biggest part of her day. She would occasionally go out for dinner, but not very often. Her favourite places were Claridges and Brook's. She preferred members' clubs because it was easier to organise security in these places than at restaurants open to the general public. Those trips out for dinner were organised by the Royal Protection Police. They could get her anywhere in London within fifteen minutes, regardless of how bad the traffic was. The only time this didn't happen was when London was gridlocked and she had a lunch date across the road at Buckingham Palace. I told her there was no way the police could clear the traffic in time for her to get to the palace, so we might have to cancel or put it off. 'Nonsense,' she said, 'We'll just have to walk.'

And off she went, with her security force in tow, across the park. There was a band playing and you could see everyone's faces gradually turn from the musicians to witness this impromptu walkabout by the most senior member of the Royal Family. It was made more remarkable by the fact that she was very rarely seen out then because of her age. When we crossed the park, we reached a pedestrian crossing and one of the personal protection officers said to her, 'I'm going to have to press the button now.'

'Oh, well, what does this button do?' she said.

'You press it,' he replied, 'and it tells you when you can cross the road.'

She turned with a look of utter astonishment on her face and whispered, 'Isn't that ingenious?'

It was one of the most fantastic things she had ever seen. But like most people her age, technology had long passed her by. If she was in a car, she never wondered how air conditioning worked, she just wound the window down if she were hot. This was a woman who existed before commercial air travel had come into being and when she was born the concept of cars was in its infancy. So to be able just to push a button to stop traffic was quite amazing to her, and also proved how sheltered her life had been.

Away from London, she loved picnic lunches at Birkhall and delighted in surprising unsuspecting couples enjoying a sandwich break as part of their walking holiday. One such couple was an Edinburgh lawyer and his wife. They had found a nice spot with a pleasant view, when suddenly behind them the whole protection unit turned up with police cars, Land Rovers, the lot. You could see the pair very occasionally having a peep round with a look of consternation on their faces to witness officers with pistols on patrol and police cars prowling less than 100 feet from where they were enjoying their tranquil break. When the Queen Mother arrived, she spotted them immediately and said, 'Oh, who do you think that is sat over there? Do we know them?'

I said, 'I don't think so, ma'am.'

'Well, go and see who it is and see what they are like. If they are nice, bring them over for a drink,' she told me.

The couple I was about to ambush were staying at a country club about 200 yards further down the hill. As I approached, they were chatting and didn't notice me at their back, so I coughed and they looked round and quickly got up.

'The Queen Mother is over there,' I said, 'She'd like to know if you want to join her for a drink.'

They looked at me, then at each other, and then back at me before the quite clearly startled lawyer said, 'The Queen Mother?'

'Yes,' I replied.

'You mean THE Queen Mother?'

'Yes,' I added.

'Well, erm, well, yes, of course, we'd love to,' he said.

So over they went to the Queen Mother, and from going on a walking holiday on their own, they were now having gin and tonic with the former Queen of England and probably sitting there thinking that nobody would ever believe it, at which point Prince Charles joined the party, having walked up from Birkhall. This completely blew their minds. They spent a good hour chatting about their favourite walks and Scotland in general before I got the nod from the Queen Mother that it was time for them to leave and, taking their glasses off them regardless of whether they were empty or not, I said, 'Right, time to go then.'

And off they popped to their country club to recount their tale, which I imagine probably to this day no one believes. Just dismissing them like that may seem a fairly brutal way of telling people to go, but one thing I found in the job was that people would often collar me at parties and ask me to give them guidance as to the correct way to depart. I simply told them, 'Don't worry; you'll know when it's time to go.'

Sure enough, when it came to leaving time, the Queen Mother went up to them and said, 'Well, it's been nice having you, bye!'

She would do this even if they had a full drink in their hand. But she wasn't being rude; she just knew people wanted a clear signal as to when they needed to depart and she was doing it the best way she possibly could, by leaving them in no doubt that it was time to go. This was no different for the Edinburgh lawyer and his wife.

The Queen Mum loved these impromptu meetings with people, because she knew it would really mean something to those who were invited to have a drink with her. She was a naturally friendly person and that's why I think she was so loved in the country as a whole.

I found lunches a breeze and made few what you might term cock-ups; until I was nearing the end of my two years, that is. It was in the early summer of 1995 and we were having dinner at the Castle of Mey. The dining room faces west, so you often get the sun streaming through the stained-glass windows and lighting up the room in an amazing rainbow of colours. It reminded me of some of the scenes in *Brideshead Revisited* but on a much grander scale, and I was dining with the Queen Mother and other guests. We had finished our main course and were on to puddings. The Queen Mother loved her stodgy puddings – bread-and-butter pudding, chocolate mousse, and rhubarb crumble with custard were her favourites. The butler, Reg, came in with a big bowl of chocolate mousse and put a huge gloop into everyone's bowl and then the shortbread came out and the chocolate sprinkles. I was in heaven, it was the best pud I had ever had and I just couldn't get enough of it. Anyway, a couple of days later, we had another meal and the same bowl came out and there was Reg again with a big smile on his face, but everyone was having tiny portions and I thought, what the hell is going on here, are people suddenly watching their calories? When Reg came around to me, I said, 'Go on, Reg, I'll have lots, please.'

'I don't think you really should,' he said.

'No, no, come on, Reg.'

And with an 'okay', he gave me a gloop, only for me to ask him, 'Any chance of another spoonful?'

Again, he said okay and dolloped another spoonful onto

my plate, and I sat there smiling while the other guests looked at me as though I was completely bonkers.

Then Reg came in with a big round of toast. I told him, 'No toast for me, Reg, I'll wait for the shortbreads to come.'

'I'd take some toast if I was you,' he said.

But I kept insisting that I would have shortbreads and Reg, in typical style, stood there and whispered, 'Take some toast,' and, hitting the bottom of the tray, popped a piece onto my plate.

I said, 'Great, thanks a bunch, Reg,' while all the time thinking, who the hell has chocolate mousse with toast?

He just winked at me and went, 'You're welcome.'

I got my spoon and stuck in, only to discover to my horror that it was warm liver and onion pâté, and I had the equivalent of about fourteen portions of it on my plate.

Panic set in: I had asked for more, so there was no way I could get out of eating it all, and there was every chance I would drop dead of a heart attack upon finishing it. But halfway through it, as my blood pressure began to rise from all the saturated fats now swilling around my body, the Queen Mother leant over and whispered to me, 'It's not what you thought it was, is it?'

I winced in embarrassment and replied, 'No, ma'am, it isn't.'

'Never mind,' she said, 'you just eat a little bit more and leave the rest.'

'Thank you, ma'am,' I replied.

Savoury puddings are an old-fashioned concept that goes back hundreds of years. One example is a thing called devils on horseback, which is bacon wrapped around prunes.

There would also be things like bacon, kidney and sausage combinations. The Queen Mother liked them because she was used to them. But for me, it did take some getting used to and, to be honest, I never really got the hang of them.

CHAPTER FOUR

WHEN IS NELSON MANDELA GOING TO STAND UP?

He lay almost flat on the floor, face down, as everyone watched and waited, and waited, and waited. The seconds ticked by, then the minutes; when was he going to stand up? I began to panic, my eyes darted to the left and right frantically. What was the etiquette here? What was the protocol for dealing with someone who stayed flat on the floor? Here was a man who had fought oppression, injustice and tyranny with such grace and bravery – who was I to tell him what to do? But the Queen Mother led everyone and looked on with calm grace. After all, in years gone by, particularly in Africa, this would have been usual and to her there was nothing unusual about this situation. Here was Nelson Mandela, the new leader of a free South Africa, lying prone before the former Queen of England. This is how it had been during her 1947 trip to South Africa. This was how she was greeted by the leaders of that country then and this is how it was now. For a few brief minutes she felt like the Queen again. She was delighted by the trip, and by the fact that South Africa was back in the Commonwealth. For despite her telling me, 'Colin, there is always fighting in Africa, it's just the way they are', and having no real forthright opinions on Apartheid, she was glad, in her words, that things 'had finally healed'.

She was very fond of Mandela and was relieved that the whole ordeal of prison and incarceration for over two decades was finally finished for him. He, on the other hand, was totally overwhelmed by the whole experience of meeting her and recognised the fact that when her husband had been King, Britain ruled the world. So this was a big moment for him and he didn't just go through the motions. When he walked in to meet her at Clarence House, I introduced him by saying 'Your Majesty, Mr Mandela.'

He was about two paces away from her and the Queen Mother put her hand out to shake his. Ordinarily, he would shake her hand and bow at the same time, but as she did this he just collapsed to the floor, and I mean *collapsed*. Everybody else was left standing there. I remember glancing at the private secretary, Sir Alastair Aird, and thinking, what do we do now, as the minutes rolled by and he was still on the floor with his face literally buried in the carpet. It was an acknowledgement that he was not worthy in her presence. But this was the President of South Africa who had won the Nobel Peace Prize for his fight against a vicious, racist regime. I remember thinking that if a man of his stature is doing this in front of the Queen Mother, what should I be doing? It was very humbling to be there. But after about four minutes, with the Queen Mother just patiently standing there acknowledging him, I was struggling a bit. What do you do when someone just flings themselves to the floor and doesn't get up? I was desperate to say, you can get up now, but there was just no precedent of etiquette laid down for a situation like this. So I just kept my mouth shut. Eventually, the Queen Mother said, 'Come on, let's go and have some tea.'

It was one of those moments where, if she hadn't said something, he might have stayed down there for a lot longer. This was a defining moment for me in seeing someone react in this way to the British Royal Family, perhaps the most powerful family in the world in terms of wealth and prestige, and I found it quite incredible. Mandela himself was unique. His enigma lay in how he defined his role as head of such a powerful nation in such a mild and, dare I say it, nice manner. He was very, very informal, but was one of those people who had an amazing aura about him, a certain kind of peacefulness. After about ten minutes chatting with him and his entourage of three, the Queen Mother and Mr Mandela went off for a private meeting where she asked him about his time in prison and he talked to her about the Commonwealth. I remember her reflecting on the visit to people and saying: 'It was quite an extraordinary trip. He just flung himself on the floor. It was quite extraordinary.'

Mandela made a huge impact on her. She was quite taken

with the fact he was just overwhelmed by it all. But she loved the Commonwealth and the historic links and memories they brought with a passion. She was in her element when receiving delegations from Australia, New Zealand, India, Africa or Canada, and one of the highlights was when South Africa was invited back into the fold. To her, Mandela's visit was a way of Britain saying to him, welcome home. The Commonwealth is the legacy of the British Empire and, for the Queen Mother, it was a link to the old world she knew before the War. She saw the Commonwealth as her last little bit of empire. So when Mandela lay prostrate on the floor, he was doing what foreign dignitaries from Africa had been doing many decades previously. This was how people reacted to her when she was with her husband, especially around the Empire and in Africa. It was totally unexpected, quite extraordinary and very, very moving.

She had her favourite countries and also ones she wasn't so keen on, which were Germany, Japan and France. She really wasn't keen at all on the Germans. It was largely because of her memories of the War with the Blitz and everything that went with it. She saw first-hand the devastating effect that the bombings had on Londoners and, in being bombed herself, felt personally attached to it. And together with the Holocaust and how prisoners-of-war, many of whom were her friends, had been treated she would often say, 'The Germans did some awful, awful things.'

But when there were Germans present, she was always gracious and polite to them. It is important that this is put into the context of not just the Second World War, but also the First, which broke out on her fourteenth birthday. By the end of 1914, her mother had turned Glamis Castle's banqueting hall into a convalescent home for wounded soldiers and Elizabeth helped looked after the patients, who were all officers. She continued this task until the War ended, prompting one soldier to write: 'For all her fifteen years she was very womanly, kind-hearted and sympathetic.'

Another soldier whom she tended wrote on a card that she should be 'Hung, drawn and quartered: hung in diamonds, drawn by the best carriages, and quartered in the finest palaces in the land'.

Amazingly, during a visit to an older sister in Suffolk, the pair overheard a dentist who lived next door plying sailors with drink and quizzing them about ship movements. They reported him to the police and he was arrested as a spy. Her future father-in-law (though she didn't know it at the time), King George V, heard of the incident, but the girls politely declined the offer of a medal.

The Japanese were another story. She thought they were even worse than the Germans and would say: 'They really were dreadful, dreadful. The indignities those poor men suffered in their hands.' She never forgot, and never allowed anybody in her presence to forget.

She didn't really mind the French, but she certainly liked to poke fun at them. She was a fluent French speaker and used to holiday there. But she was scathing about the fact that they gave up during World War II. She would say, 'How could you be beaten if you didn't want to be beaten?' She firmly believed that, unlike the French, Britain did the right thing because it stood its ground, and France barely put up a fight, when they should have fought down to the very last man against such awful tyranny. She would sometimes say: 'We bailed the French out, you know.' So she expected more from them because Britain saved their skin. She was even more scathing about the fact that many years later, the French President, de Gaulle, vetoed our entry into the then EEC. She didn't think that was on at all. She often said, 'Of course, we don't really like the French, do we, Colin?' and would jokingly pre-empt comments with things like 'Oh, the French would say that, wouldn't they?' and 'Oh, the French are a funny lot'.

She often bantered about them. It was all very friendly, but I do remember Jacques Chirac coming to visit Clarence House for afternoon tea with an entourage of about ten people – why so many, I do not know, because most leaders brought two or three with them and I had great difficulty working out who was my opposite number. There were so many that we had to draft in some of the ladies-in-waiting to talk to them. All through their meeting, which lasted about half an hour, the Queen Mother was very feisty. I remember her responding to a comment that the President made with 'Oh, you French would like that, wouldn't you?' which I found funny, but although they laughed, I wasn't so sure they fully appreciated it. They were a bit self-conscious and didn't really know how to respond to comments like that. I could tell the French President was slightly nervy in her presence. But it wasn't super-formal, like a visit to the prime minister. This was tea and buns and a chat. It was very sociable and much more relaxed.

Virtually every leader of importance who came to visit Britain made a trip to Clarence House. After all, how could they not pay a visit to the old Queen of England? Especially the French with whom there are so many historic links, despite the jokes. Although the War wasn't mentioned during the French visit, there was every chance she would have brought it up if they had stayed longer. She did mention to them her love of the Special Forces, and particularly the SOE, but it wasn't dwelt on. Afterwards she expressed with some humour the fact that the French delegation needed such a high security presence. She didn't really think about her own personal safety and would have quite happily attended events without any security whatsoever. But no one really thought for a second that anyone would try to bump off the Queen Mother. And while security was tight, the Queen Mother remained quietly detached from perceived threats and security alerts. She reminded me of the colonel in *Apocalypse Now* walking along the beach, with explosions going off all around. She too had this air of indestructibility about her and I felt, even when we were meeting the public at large gatherings, which could have proven to be a security risk, that as long as I was with her there was no way I would ever be in danger. She was just not the sort of target anyone would actually want to hit – and the negative press would have killed off any individual or group who tried to do it. Of course, there were worries surrounding groups such as the IRA, who were still very active then. But she was cynical towards them and would say, 'Oh, they really are very naughty and very, very confused. The whole thing is such a mess.'

Her one concession to security was the presence of her night-time policeman, Tony George, who was past regular police retirement age. He had special dispensation to be armed past the age of sixty-five, and was in his seventies when I worked at Clarence House. Basically, he just sat outside the Queen Mother's door all night and followed her everywhere she went during the dark hours. He would come in to start at about 10.00 pm and if, say, at Birkhall, I got up in the middle of the night to go for a wee or for a midnight snack, up would pop Tony with his gun checking what was going on. He was very on the ball. His shift finished at breakfast.

Visits by foreign dignitaries were viewed by them as a bit of a jolly because the Queen Mother had a way of dispelling the air of formality that surrounded the trip, so everyone could be themselves. This particularly applied to various MPs who would come for lunch, such as Henry Bellingham or Lord Strathmore, the then chief whip. Her political leanings tended very much towards the Tories and very much with Margaret Thatcher. The Queen Mother was a Thatcherite through and through and loved her no-nonsense approach, especially towards the Falklands War and the way she dealt with that. She would say to me about the Argentine invasion: 'They took our island and we got them; it's as simple as that.'

Thatcher really did impress her because she liked people

with convictions and people who believed in what they did. To the Queen Mother's mind, if you believed in your convictions you could pretty much do anything. She saw in Thatcher a woman who was substance over style and would say to me: 'I do like Margaret Thatcher. She was very good for the country because she was strong as a leader, knew what she wanted and got on with it.'

To her, that was what life was all about; telling people you were going to do something, doing it and getting on with things, and the whole concept of the Falklands and Thatcher's reaction to being invaded was marvellous. The Queen Mother felt that the country pulled together and did its duty. She didn't want any part of Britain to be invaded and believed in defending it right down to the last man or woman if the circumstances warranted it. So Thatcher's strength of character and leadership struck a chord with her rather like Winston Churchill's did during World War II. She was fond of Churchill in very much the same way as Thatcher. She saw in him that spark which says, I'm going to go in and sort this mess out, and told me, 'Winston was just what the country needed during the War. He was the perfect leader.'

After the War, I think she felt he had had his time and stayed on for a bit too long. However, during hostilities she saw him as the perfect tonic. But her favourite politician was definitely Thatcher, whom she talked about much more than Winston. She once told me, 'Margaret Thatcher is very much like Winston, but she's just got that little bit extra.'

The whole Maggie thing was something of an enigma for her simply because she was a woman in a position of power which, initially, the Queen Mother viewed as a bit odd. But she liked the fact she was strong and that they shared similar views. The Queen Mother was Tory through and through, there's no doubt about that.

She didn't like all Conservatives, though. She found John Major dull. He just wasn't on her radar. To appear on her radar, you had to do something. You didn't even have to be accomplished. You had to be memorable. John Major simply didn't fit the bill. He was merely the prime minister and that was that, although she would have found his dalliance with Edwina Currie highly amusing, I'm sure.

She mentioned Tony Blair quite a few times, but only for the fact that he smiled a lot, and she did impressions of him where she would break into this huge grin and be all teeth. She did find it quite amusing that he was always smiling for no apparent reason. And she found New Labour to be very much old Conservative and would say to me: 'It's now almost impossible to differentiate between the two parties.'

Blair, to her, was a Conservative and that pleased her in one way, but she summed him up in his smile as being style over substance and said to me that she found him 'all teeth and no bite'.

But Blair and Major may want to take solace from the fact that overall the Queen Mother liked male company and despite all the comings and goings of heads of state, she felt most comfortable in a room full of military people, having spent most of her life surrounded by people from the forces. She didn't like the kind of society chit-chat that socialite women had. She liked to talk about military matters, current affairs and sports, such as horse racing, fishing, shooting and hunting. She actually fly-fished until she was about seventy-five and was a great field sports person in general. So the whole concept of having a wives' afternoon talking about crochet or something like that really didn't appeal to her. Male company she found to be a bit sharper.

A good example of her aversion to members of the female sex was when she went on walkabouts and she'd describe women 'thrusting babies at me'. They automatically assumed she loved babies; it was not that she disliked them, but she couldn't understand why people felt the need for her to handle them. Even at Sandringham, when she went down to the annual flower show, she would say, 'There were lots of people there today, and of course there was the thrusting of many babies.'

It wasn't something she liked, but when she described it, she did have a smile on her face, so she found it mildly amusing. She was very good at observing how people were with her without actually giving much back in the way of a comment. Whenever in doubt, she would smile broadly and move on. Her attitude to most women was that they were a bit fluffy and scatty in their ways. This didn't include her ladies-in-waiting though; they were hand-picked because they were very three-dimensional and interesting people, especially the senior lady-in-waiting, Dame Frances Campbell-Preston, who was one of the Queen Mother's closest friends. After lunch, the pair of them would often stay and talk alone and they talked more as friends than formal acquaintances. The Queen Mother was at her most emotional when talking to her ladies-in-waiting. She would let herself go a little bit and I detected as I left the room that they would be getting into a proper conversation. Of all the staff, the ladies-in-waiting had this special bond with her, but as for any other females, there was a distinct level of tolerance applied.

She didn't really have what I would term best friends in the conventional sense and she had been widowed for over forty years when I joined her, so it would be a fair assumption to think she could have been lonely at Clarence House. But if she were lonely, she hid it very well. She never really talked about the King, though there were lots of portraits and paintings of him on the walls of her London home, so he couldn't have been far from her thoughts. They met for the first time at a ball in May 1920 and by the end of the evening the then Prince Albert – a shy young man who had a terrible stammer – had fallen in love with her. But she didn't make it easy for him. He pursued her for three years and she twice turned down marriage proposals which protocol demanded were made to her through intermediaries. On one famous occasion she told the messenger her reason for declining Albert's hand in marriage was that she was 'afraid never, never again to be free to speak and act as I feel I really ought to'.

When the Prince declared he would marry no other, his mother, Queen Mary, visited Glamis to see at first hand the woman who had stolen her son's heart. She then arranged for a love rival, the Earl of Moray, to be dispatched to an overseas post, clearing the Prince's way and when, on the third time, in 1923, he ignored protocol and asked her directly, she accepted. They married at Westminster Abbey in the same year. On the way out of the Abbey Elizabeth laid her bouquet at the Tomb of the Unknown Warrior, a gesture that has been echoed by every royal bride since; their bouquets are taken back to the Abbey and laid at the tomb just inside the West Door. She still had her wedding dress at Clarence House when I was there. Their honeymoon was spent at Polesden Lacey, a manor house in Surrey, and at the Queen Mother's ancestral home, Glamis Castle, in Scotland. Three years after they wed they had their first child, Elizabeth Alexandra Mary, now Queen Elizabeth II. Princess Margaret followed in 1930.

But, in 1936, their blissful existence was shattered by the death of King George V. When Albert's brother, King Edward VIII, decided he was going to marry the twice-divorced, American socialite Wallis Simpson, he had to abdicate and Albert and his wife suddenly became King and Queen of England, with Albert taking the title of King George VI. The coronation took place on 12 May 1937. Their popularity soared to stratospheric levels during the Second World War, when they visited bombed areas of the East End of London and other parts of the country and they invented the concept of the royal walkabout. The Queen Mother was described by one American newspaper at this time as the 'Minister for Morale'. But seven years after the war ended, the King died of lung cancer, aged only fifty-six, and his daughter Elizabeth acceded to the throne and protocol demanded that the Queen Mother be known as the Queen Dowager. She withdrew from public life after her husband's death and even contemplated remaining out of the public spotlight forever, but was persuaded by the then prime minister, Winston Churchill, that she still had a role to play. He gave her the title Queen Elizabeth, the Queen Mother, and she threw herself into a series of engagements in the UK and toured many countries around her beloved Commonwealth. But throughout time, she felt that the loss of her husband could be laid firmly at the door of Wallis Simpson, blaming her for his early death. When comforting a friend who had lost her loved one, she was asked if it got any better with the passage of time. She replied, 'It doesn't get any better, but you get better at it.'

And that comment wonderfully sums up how she was during my two years with her. She was one of those people who were so socially skilled, they could talk to you for two hours and basically say nothing and then drop just one brief comment in and it would tell you everything you needed to know. She would never reveal anything for a second more than she needed to. You never heard her say 'Oh, I'm sad'. Instead, she would use the term 'Isn't it sad'.

That's why it was virtually impossible to pierce her skin and get to the real woman. Occasionally, she would bring up the subject of her late husband and mention a trip with him to South Africa in 1947 – the same trip on which an Afrikaner said to her that he could never forgive the English for conquering the Boers and she, smiling, replied, 'Oh, I understand that perfectly. We feel very much the same in Scotland.' She still had this amazingly detailed memory of every aspect of the trip recalling everything perfectly, including going to visit these various tribal chiefs and how they reacted when they were given MBEs and OBEs by the King. She told me, 'Their faces just lit up. It was quite amazing to witness.' She also talked about the heat and said, 'It was almost unbearably hot,' and then she moved on.

So it obviously made a deep impression on her, as did most of her foreign trips. She described a 1939 royal tour of Canada as 'an event that was the making of us'. But she was not one of those people whom you could keep probing about these things. You couldn't really ask if she was lonely or missing the King. She had been married to a king and that was it for her when he died. Male companionship was how she sought solace and I would say that the relationship between her and Ralph was very close, but it was nothing more than companionship between two like-minded people. She summed up her views on life as 'Never complain, never explain', and this saw her through many private sorrows and personal difficulties.

The only person I think she did feel some sort of affection and love towards was her press secretary Sir Martin Gilliat. He occupied a strange position that was never officially sanctioned and he died aged eighty in 1993, shortly before I arrived at Clarence House. He was a larger-than-life character by all accounts, who had served in the King's Royal Rifle Corps and was captured four times during the War, escaping on three occasions. The last time he was caught, he was locked up in Colditz, which may have something to do with the fact that he was very eccentric and 'out there'. Some of the staff at Clarence House would say to me, 'Oh, you should've seen him, he was unbelievable.'

The Queen Mother had a soft spot for Martin. He was charming and very funny with it, too; something that appealed to the Queen Mum. When they went to the Castle of Mey for her annual holiday, he took some guests on a trip to the Orkney Islands and got talking to two Germans who said, 'Have you ever been to Germany?'

Quick as a flash he replied, 'Yes I have, actually. I stayed at a marvellous hotel and they looked after me magnificently. In fact, they wouldn't let me leave! I was given good meals, lots of exercise and plenty of fresh air.'

The Germans said, 'Ah, really. What was the name of this place?'

'Colditz,' he said.

And of course the Germans were totally flustered and didn't know where to put themselves.

Another favourite story about him that was recounted to me took place in Scotland. It was evening and dinner had finished, and the Queen Mother and the ladies had retired to another room to discuss their own things, leaving Martin and the other men to smoke cigars. Eventually, after about an hour, the gentlemen decided to join the ladies, who took it upon themselves to hide behind the curtains and pretend they weren't there. On entering the room Martin cried: 'Oh, thank f★★★ for that, they've gone to bed.'

Of all the staff, I think the Queen Mother missed him the most. They say she was never the same woman after he died and if Ralph occupied a big part in her life, Martin occupied an even bigger part in her heart.

CHAPTER FIVE

'WILL ONE OF YOU OLD QUEENS BRING THIS OLD QUEEN A GIN AND TONIC?'

One of the most famous anecdotes involving the Queen Mother was when she purportedly shouted to her staff, 'Will one of you old queens bring this old queen a gin and tonic?'

I cannot vouch for its authenticity, but after spending two years at the Queen Mother's side, I can say with some authority that I doubt she ever did say this, it just wasn't her style. But it does sum up William, known affectionately as Backstairs Billy, and Reg very well. They were in many ways like a pair of old queens. Not in a derogatory way – but they were gentle, discreet, very sensitive and caring, if a little camp with it. If surviving lunch in a sober state could be an occasional ordeal, then getting on the wrong side of these two could be lethal. Of the two, it was William, a storekeeper's son from Birtley in County Durham, who was the most famous and the longest-serving member of her household when she died. His first post was as a junior assistant in the Steward's Room at Buckingham Palace and he slowly rose through the ranks to become the Queen Mother's page. For this the Queen rewarded him by making him a member of the Royal Victorian Order. He had been at the Palace ever since he was sixteen years old, after writing a letter to the King asking for a post. He was given one in 1951. William was a larger-than-life figure and very eccentric. He was very vocal, not shy and retiring in the least. As a butler, he had this gravitas about him and he would use it to almost dive at you and say 'Sir, can I get you a drink?'

He had plenty of confidence and he knew the job inside out, never said anything that was out of turn and never crossed anyone. However, if you crossed him you would know about it. Not so much in what he said, but in what he didn't say or do. He was quite flamboyant. If he simply said 'yes' to a question and went about his work quietly, it was a fair bet he actually disagreed with you. He knew what the Queen Mother liked and disliked. He played to that and was quite willing to trip you up on protocol if he felt you had slighted him. It could be as simple as not warning you of an impending problem that you could trip yourself up over. You would then feel bad because you had made a mistake. But he was not randomly uncooperative. He would generally react to what was presented.

Guests invited for lunch who were rude or patronising to him would find that the taxi ordered for after lunch might only be able to park outside the gates of St James's Palace rather than come to the door, or perhaps no taxis might be available. At any rate, if William reacted, there was usually a good reason and he was one of the few people who could get away with it. But underneath all the pomp and duty, he was a gentle and solid character. His priority was to the Queen Mother. I got on well with him. We had this professional relationship where, although he was my junior in position, he had a greater advantage over me because of his vast experience, and I would pull rank with him at my peril. Occasionally, I would criticise him because he was wrong on certain matters of etiquette and he accepted that, and sometimes the Queen Mother would pull him up if she felt he was going beyond what the job required of him. I remember one example of this which occurred on her birthday in August 1995. She always came out of Clarence House on her birthday to wave to the crowds, accept gifts of flowers and presents and watch the Irish Guards' Band march past. That year, she was having trouble walking as her hip was playing up, which is what it was prone to do at that time. William put his arm out for her to hang on to while she walked. She looked at him with a steely gaze and her eyes narrowed as she said, 'No, I will hold on to the equerry.'

In her eyes, he had just overstepped the mark. And her rules dictated that only when she asked for someone to take her arm was that person able to take it. So she put William in his place and gave him a stare that would have turned lesser men to stone. But she held nothing against him; in fact, she was very fond of him – it was just a question of propriety. He was annoyed, though. I could see it in his face.

He had been told off, but he couldn't argue with her because she was right.

Away from work, William was much the same character, only more concentrated. It was no secret that he was gay and once or twice I saw him coming back to the lodge at Clarence House, where he lived, with a male friend, usually someone much younger than him. He might be a little tipsy, but again he managed to carry it off with great presence and humour. He could best be described as jovial in these moments. But even out of hours, he would dress very smartly in immaculate suits, often at least as well made as the ones the private secretary wore and his were top of the range. With William, there was the strong, quiet and incredibly discreet character that was ever so polite, and there was the side of him away from work; a person who was very much his own man and who could get a little bit raucous. This also showed at work from time to time as he sought to grab the limelight at every opportunity. Often when the Queen Mother was out and about and there were cameras around, he would be in the picture making sure he was standing close by. You could tell by watching the way he operated that he loved his role and everything that went with it. He really was in his element. Most of all, he was devoted to the Queen Mother and that earned him everyone's respect. The saddest aspect of his life came when the Queen Mother died. He was asked to leave his garden lodge at Clarence House and was dismissed. It was simply not right, and after fifty years of loyal service, many felt that he should have been offered another position in the household. It wasn't like leaving ICI or some limited company; this was a family he had worked for and had given up a significant amount of his time to serve. I think the Queen Mother would have been disappointed at the way he was booted out. In some ways, his leaving was a surprise, although in another, he may have upset a lot of people over the years. The best comparison I can make is with the book and the film *Get Shorty*, in the sense that while Momo is alive nothing will happen to Chilly Palmer. While the Queen Mother was alive, William was protected, but once she had gone, he was yesterday's man.

Reg Wilcox, the lesser known but equally senior butler, began his Royal service in 1954 as a Buckingham Palace footman and came to Clarence House in 1960. He was totally different to William. He was kinder, calmer and much more cheerful; in fact, he was one of the nicest human beings you could ever wish to meet. He was full of jokes and observations, silly asides and funny comments. I remember one day I had run out of socks – they were all dirty, apart from a pair of bright orange ones, which were probably a Christmas present. So I came to work wearing one of my usual suits and these garish socks and, as I was sitting at my desk, Reg walked past the doorway carrying a tea tray. I thought he hadn't even seen me, but a second or two after he passed, he re-appeared, this time walking backwards, beamed at me and said, 'Love the socks!' It was pure comedy.

He was the sort of man who never treated life too seriously, and he would draw everybody into his light-hearted way of viewing things; even the Queen Mother was charmed by him. There was an incident where Reg cut himself on a gate in Scotland and said in a very over-the-top and affected manner, 'Does this family want my blood?'

Quick as a flash, the Queen Mother replied, 'No, just your sweat and tears.'

One thing that both William and Reg definitely shared was their love of the Queen Mother. They always talked about her in tones of great reverence and affection: even when they were up against it and the Queen Mother would be saying to them, 'No, no, no, you do it this way', they would always show the correct manner to her and never overstepped protocol.

In their eyes, she was a higher authority than the Queen. She was the ultimate royal and they worked bloody hard to make sure her daily routine was as comfortable as possible, starting very early in the morning, before 7.00 on most days, making sure that the rest of the staff were doing what they were supposed to be doing and then organising their team of junior butlers, who wore red as opposed to the black outfits worn by William and Reg, for the day ahead. During lunch, they would serve the wine and the junior butlers did the food. This in itself could cause problems, if they decided they wanted to have a bit of fun with you. One of their many tricks was filling and refilling your glass with wine throughout the meal, knowing that if you were sitting there with a full glass the Queen Mother would say, 'Come on, drink up.'

I often got caught out by this. One of them would be saying something to me and while I turned to speak to them, the other one would be filling my glass to the brim.

This would continue throughout the meal and there were times when I walked out of lunch well on the way to being completely blotto.

Another trick they would use, which was picked up and adopted by other members of staff, was throwing their weight to make sure they got their way. They would say: 'Her Majesty would like it done this way.'

You couldn't really argue with them about that, but on the other hand who were they to say what the Queen Mother wanted, or didn't want? To me, it was a gross misuse of the Queen Mother's name. But it was hard to ignore because you could never be one hundred per cent certain whether the Queen Mother did actually want it done that way, or whether it was a ruse to get their own way. No one to this day will ever know.

Beneath William and Reg were the junior butlers, of whom there were seven, on and off. Most of them only stayed two or three years before trading in on the fact that they had worked for the most famous family in the world to go and serve a Hollywood film star or some major businessman living somewhere far more exotic than Central London. Upon leaving the Household, many of them joined a company called Greycoats, which was an employment agency taking on a lot of ex-Palace staff. They found domestic staff for the rich and famous; for example, one senior butler called Stephen Cheetham, who had been at Clarence House for over ten years, left to take up a dream job in Monaco, being paid considerably more than I had earned as the equerry. He spent six months of the year looking after an unattended house and for the other six months acted as personal assistant to his employer. Before that he was on a much more modest salary working for the Queen Mother.

So there was a rapid turnover of staff which meant that William and Reg sometimes had quite a job enforcing standards and discipline among the younger ones. It was quite obvious to any of the minor staff that William and Reg would be in the job until they died so chances of promotion were virtually non-existent. Reg, who was in his seventies, worked until two days before he died from leukaemia and it was only his sense of duty and loyalty to the Queen Mother that kept him going. She had something magical and magisterial about her. She was selfless and at the same time untouchable, as opposed to, say, her grandson Charles, who happens to be royal, and one with opinions that many people don't always see eye to eye with.

William and Reg were a team, albeit an eccentric one. I would often find that because there were two of them they could get a bit touchy if you asked one for something without asking the other. William often felt put out if I asked Reg something, so you really did have to tip-toe around them. But after a few months at Clarence House, I realised that the more senior the staff were, then the less you had to worry about insecurities of position and rank. So people like the private secretary, the treasurer and the ladies-in-waiting were easy-going and very friendly. But the further away you got from the royal epicentre, the more affected some people became. They would constantly worry about their status and try to trip you up, so you had to be careful. For example, if I went into the private secretary's office and said to Alastair that I needed to take the day off, he'd say, 'Oh, fine, just make sure your in-tray is empty.' But secretaries below him might say, 'Oh, well, that's not on,' and immediately they'd find something for me to get involved in.

So I really was on my guard at all times because the less power some staff found they had, the more they needed to show the power they actually did have. But of course this happens everywhere. However, if I was wary of them, then they were very wary of the treasurer Sir Ralph Anstruther. As I noted earlier, he was a stickler for detail and was constantly picking people up on the state of their ties or their shoes, but it was purely on a professional level – though some of the other staff didn't seem to think so – and he was always immaculately turned out. He was quietly kind, although most of the previous equerries thought him an ogre, and he was fond of people, especially those who kept up the high standards he set himself. Once I realised this, I found him a great man to work for. His attention to the minutiae also rubbed off on the Queen Mother, who would say to me, 'Oh, don't move the napkins or Ralph will get upset.'

She would sometimes say this in his presence just to be a bit naughty. But everyone to a man saw him as super-strict. He operated like a senior military figure. Yet his comments on girls' skirts were his way of telling me that there was a spark there, and that he was human after all. And if, on occasion, I hadn't polished my shoes, I would get round it by saying, 'Look, Ralph, I'm really sorry about the state of my shoes. I realise they're dirty and I'll do something about them straight away.'

He would be happy that I had recognised this, but if I hadn't mentioned them, he would be horrified. It would be as if I didn't care and then he would be even more on guard because he would feel standards were beginning to slip. It was the same with the Queen Mother. She didn't mind if a member of staff made a mistake because she recognised that everyone made them, it was human nature. What she didn't tolerate was unkindness or general sloppiness.

Ralph was a courtier very much from a different century and had served in the Queen Mother's household since the 1950s. He was her equerry from 1959, assistant private secretary from 1959 to 1964 and treasurer from 1961. By the time I arrived, he had blended his work role perfectly with that of companion to the Queen Mother. In a way, he was rather like her in the sense that technology had passed him by. I remember once when he was in my car on a hot day and I put the air conditioning on. He wound down the window and I said, 'Ralph, you can't do that. The air conditioning won't work.'

'Rubbish,' he replied. 'If you want cold air, you get it from outside,' and he insisted on having the window wound down, so I just turned the air conditioning off and we suffered.

He was certainly a real stickler for detail. Whenever the Queen Mother went abroad, Ralph would go on a reconnaissance mission to wherever she was visiting, briefing her hosts on her likes and dislikes and ensuring that she encountered nothing she didn't want to, and above all making sure they were well stocked up with her favourite gin. But when I arrived he was seventy-two years old, had been serving at Clarence House for nearly forty years and time was catching up with him. I had missed him in his prime and I regretted that in some ways. Once, during a picnic lunch in Scotland, he fell asleep, which, if it had been any other person, would have been deemed a major breach of protocol. But this was an old man who had had a stroke and the Queen Mother simply said, 'Come on, let's just clear up around him and he'll wake up eventually.'

When he did wake up, he was a bit embarrassed, but the Queen Mother was adamant that nobody should tell him what happened as it would make him feel uncomfortable and probably upset him even more. Certainly, he commanded total respect from all the younger royals: Charles, Anne, Andrew and Edward. He had helped to bring them up and when Charles was younger, Ralph took him down to the railway lines in Scotland and they put pennies on the track for the trains to crush. He would tell me these stories and I would be amazed. Occasionally in life, you meet people who are so not of this world that they seem the most interesting people on earth and this was Ralph through and through. He was a master of etiquette, who wasn't above grabbing hold of the private secretary and saying, 'I say, dear boy, your tie is done up incorrectly' or, 'I see you haven't shone your shoes before coming here.'

It was a major coup for me when I took Ralph out for the day at Sandringham and he actually went into a pub, ate fish and chips and took his jacket off. For a start, he would never usually be seen dead in a pub and to this day I have no idea why he agreed to go in with me. And then his taking his jacket off was the biggest surprise ever. In his eyes, a gentleman never took his jacket off, whatever the weather, because if he did, he would be incorrectly dressed. I was amazed. He was effectively kicking off his shoes and, possibly for the first time in decades, actually relaxing. But etiquette was his forte. If guests came to Clarence House for lunch, he would whisper things to me such as: 'That man over there is wearing brown shoes. You should always wear black shoes for formal occasions.' Alternatively, he might say, 'Look at that person over there. He is constantly talking over the other people around him. Never do that. Always let people finish what they are saying.' Something I could still learn!

I always remember Ralph giving me these tips. Once, when I was at a Clarence House dinner party, I was talking to someone and they mentioned something, so I ran off to get a pen and paper to write it down. Afterwards, Ralph took me to one side and said, 'Colin, never write anything down during a party. That is not the done thing. You must wait until afterwards.'

He had problems adjusting to the more liberal aspects of modern life. As treasurer, it was Ralph's job to sign a lot of the Queen Mother's personal cheques and to look after her finances and make sure spending didn't get out of control. He also laid the Queen Mother's wreath at the Cenotaph on Remembrance Sunday. The Royal Family, and especially the Queen Mother, never worried about money and never got too over-excited about accumulation of wealth. They just got on with things and people like Ralph handled the cash side. The Queen Mother never carried money and would never get into a situation where she needed to produce it; Ralph, as her money man, was the consummate courtier who was very professional and would discreetly arrange payment for things when the Queen Mother was out of earshot.

At the end of each working day, I went home, kicked off my shoes, put on jeans and a T-shirt and would pop off to the supermarket or something like that. But when Ralph went back to his three-bedroom London home – he also had a huge house in Scotland – he would stay in exactly the same mode as he did at Clarence House and still wear a stiff collar. I never saw him without a tie on. He just couldn't switch out of Queen Mother mode, which was very formal, very reserved, quiet and respectful, but busy, and Ralph, even at home, was busy. I'm not sure how he kept it up because there were times I would go back to my flat absolutely exhausted. The only time Ralph really switched off was when *Casualty* was on television – he loved that programme.

But the job really was his life and consumed his every minute. He didn't give it up, even after his second stroke, which happened towards the end of my service. He just carried on. Sadly, the second stroke floored him – you would find him coming in on a Saturday thinking it was a work day. It got to the stage where he just couldn't do the job. But because he had worked there for close on half a century nobody was going to fire him, least of all the Queen Mother, who regarded him as one of her closest companions and possibly the most loyal who had ever worked for her. Ralph didn't even draw a salary. He had his own private income and he did the job not for any sort of prestige, but out of a sense of duty. He gave up his life to look after the Queen Mother. Some people reading this will think what a waste of a life but to me it was a very noble thing to do. I couldn't have done it. After two years working there, I felt I had done my bit when the time came. If the Queen Mother had asked me to stay on, it would have put me in a difficult position, but I would have left because I wanted to get on with my own life. But people like Ralph, and to a certain extent William and Reg, are a dying breed. They are almost like nurses doing what they do as a vocation rather than for any reward. These days, it's rare to do anything out of a sense of duty but these guys did it every day of their lives and the Queen Mother respected them for it. After Ralph had his second stroke, she insisted that he came to live at Clarence House. He couldn't really function at all, but the staff would work out ways to make him feel as if he were still doing his job, and that was how the Queen Mother wanted it. He had helped her, now she wanted to help him through his illness.

I was the only equerry ever to visit him at his family seat, Balcaskie House in Pittenweem, in Fife, which had belonged at one time to Robert the Bruce. The house was so old the glass in the windows had run and melted to the bottom so the window panes were thicker at the bottom than they were at the top. The place was huge and had about thirty bedrooms. As you entered, you came into a huge round chamber with pictures of Ralph's ancestors on the wall and various relics including a bamboo cane that his uncle had kept after fighting in the Chindit expeditions into Burma. As I came in, his hand swept around the room to the pictures and he said, 'Meet the folks.'

Ralph, who was the 7th Baronet of Balcaskie, had a housekeeper called Margaret, who was older than he; I think she was about eighty-five. She had looked after him ever since he was a baby, but she was now so frail I thought she would snap at any moment. But she was there to cook and serve dinner, or so I thought. As I sat at the table waiting for the food to be served, I could see Margaret through the wooden hatch sitting in the kitchen. Ralph and I were at either end of a huge table. Suddenly, Ralph said, 'Ah, Margaret, I think we are ready for our dinner now.'

She replied: 'Okay, Sir Ralph.'

At that point, Ralph jumped out of his chair, ran into the kitchen, picked up all the plates and put them on or near the serving hatch. He then ran round to the other side, picked up the plates from the serving hatch and put them on the table, before sitting down and saying 'Thank you, Margaret'. To which, Margaret replied, 'Thank you, Sir Ralph,' and shut the kitchen door!

When we had finished our starters, Ralph said, 'Margaret, I think we are ready.'

This was her signal to open the kitchen doors and he jumped up again, picked up all the plates and put them on the hatch. He then ran into the kitchen, picked up the plates from the hatch and put them in the dishwasher. Margaret just stood there and watched the whole thing because she was now too frail to do much save for opening and closing doors. But by her doing this they were still going through the motions of the master–servant relationship that they had had all their lives. She was now too old so he did everything on her behalf. It was one of the most beautiful things I have ever seen. Here was this upper-class, former major with the British Army who wanted to do everything right, yet doing all of the work of his housekeeper because he cared about her so deeply, and doing it in a way that meant neither lost face. It was very similar to the relationship he had with the Queen Mother towards the end of his life. She helped him after he had his strokes by allowing him to assume the cloak of treasurer, even though it no longer really fitted him; she still wanted him to know that the game was being played right up to the end because he wouldn't have wanted it any other way. He died in May 2002, aged eighty. I was deeply saddened but also very aware that he had lived a fuller and more rewarding life than a thousand people you could pick at random.

I had heard tales of how, after the Second World War, he was posted to Malaya to fight the Communists and almost drowned when he slipped on a stone and was carried away by a river. It took a guardsman to plunge in after him and save his life. Ironically, although Ralph's life had been saved, he was seen as the best swimmer in the battalion. During those years, Ralph attracted women from across Europe. He was dashing, handsome and debonair. He took to walking the streets of some of the most chic capitals in Europe dressed in a white planter's suit and Panama hat. But he never married and after retiring from the Army in the mid 1950s he came to Clarence House. When he was made treasurer, he ruled the royal purse in very austere fashion and was a firm believer in bulk buying, often carrying shopping baskets piled high with jars of instant coffee and the like back to Clarence House. Even at Balcaskie, he maintained this air of frugality. He made his own jam, which often graced the Queen Mother's breakfast table, and bulk bought baked beans and other items in a bid to save money. He fully justified his orders: CVO in 1967, KCVO in 1976, and GCVO in 1992. When he retired in 1998, he was made Treasurer Emeritus to the Queen Mother, which was a fitting tribute to a life lived to the full.

Senior to Ralph's position was that of private secretary, which was held by Sir Alastair Aird. He was in effect the managing director of the household and oversaw virtually everything about the Queen Mother's life. Like me, he joined Clarence House as the Queen Mother's equerry in 1960. By 1994, he was seen as her right-hand man and was expected to stay in this position until either he, or she, died. It was kind of an unwritten rule. Because the Queen Mother undertook royal duties and hadn't retired, even in her nineties, none of the other staff felt they could go into retirement, least of all Alastair. Technically, this ex-Army officer held the senior position within the household, but Ralph, as a GCVO, held the senior title. Alastair was very straightforward, calm, organised and reliable. You could sometimes be mistaken for thinking he was just a bit aloof, but he was very worldly, and had his feet firmly on the ground. More so than Ralph, who lived in a kind of nineteenth-century bubble.

Alastair was my daily contact as equerry. The first thing I did in the morning was to go into my office, check my diary and go and see him to talk through the day. He was always very calm and matter of fact about things and had a conversational manner about him. One of his biggest strengths was that he knew all the staff very well and how the intricacies and delicate balances between different characters worked. It was Alastair who put me right when I had the problem with the chauffeur. Within the household, Alastair was known as the guru of etiquette and protocol, in a different way to Ralph. Alastair was more officious and knew all the rules concerning how to address people and how to write letters correctly, that sort of thing. He also acted as my technical mentor, constantly advising me on how things should be done correctly. This was a man who could look at a plan, for example, for a visit to a factory, and see problems that no one else could spot. Sometimes, he would go as far as to say 'Forget the whole thing', and simply cancel an event for that day because it had been ill thought through.

He could weigh up a situation, perhaps for a visit to a restaurant, and immediately decide whether or not it was appropriate for the Queen Mother to go, and he would do this in a split second. He had to because she got invited to so many things. On one occasion when we were having lunch in the Green Room, the Queen Mother brought up the subject of the Post Office Tower and said, 'There used to be a restaurant in the Post Office Tower. Do you think it's still there?'

That small comment effectively meant, get us booked in this week. I said, 'I'll find out for you, ma'am.'

The problem was that even if the restaurant were closed, which I was later told it had been for years, the merest hint that the Queen Mother was to pay them a visit would have had them opening it like a shot and at an expense so vast that it would far exceed the merits of the visit, and probably warrant a few scathing paragraphs in the national tabloids to boot.

So, after lunch, Alastair grabbed me and said, 'I don't think her Majesty realises that the restaurant closed down twenty years ago. It would be better if we didn't organise a visit there. It might cause a bit of a fuss.'

With these simple instructions I didn't bother enquiring about it, but sure enough, a couple of days later, the Queen Mother said, 'How is it looking with our visit to the Post Office Tower?'

I had to say: 'I'm sorry, ma'am, but it's not open anymore.'

That was one of the amazing things about the Queen Mother, though; even into her nineties, she never forgot anything whether it was days, weeks or months later. She would always remind you of it.

During another garden lunch, the Queen Mother casually started telling me about the tunnels that exist under London. Some run from Clarence House to Buckingham Palace and from there to the Houses of Parliament. She said to me, 'Colin, bring in a torch one day and you and I should go down and explore.'

Of course, I was amazed by the idea. I didn't know anything

of the sort existed, but Alastair quickly interjected and said, 'Oh, I wouldn't bother doing that if I were you, Colin. I'm sorry, ma'am, but the tunnels closed many years ago.'

It still intrigues me as to the labyrinths that exist below the Palaces. What I do know is that the Queen Mother occasionally explored the lower levels of Buckingham Palace with the King, because she told me. She said, 'It was just after the War and we went down to the basement more out of curiosity than anything else. When we reached the basement, there was a man, I think he was a Geordie. He'd been there for a while and was very courteous to us.'

Then she added with a chuckle, 'As it turned out he didn't have a role at Clarence House at all. He was just a friend of a friend who lived in the basement. He was very polite though. I wonder what happened to him.'

I just kept thinking that would never happen these days, and what a sad world it is that it wouldn't. There was so much more innocence then which has been lost now. That's probably why Alastair was so quick to torpedo her wanting to go back down and have another look.

He was also vital in giving me the inside loop on staff issues, especially the deterioration in Ralph's health. I remember going into his office one morning and him saying, 'Look, Ralph is going to come in and ask you about going to Sandringham. Now he has got it into his head that we are going to Sandringham next week and won't have it any other way. So you can't tell him we are not going. All I want you to do when he mentions it is to say to him that everything is booked.'

Sure enough, Ralph came in and said, 'Ah, Colin, is everything in place for going to Sandringham next week?'

'Yes, everything is booked,' I replied.

'Ah, marvellous,' he said, 'Marvellous.'

Alastair gave me a look which said, thank goodness for that.

He was also good as a guide to what and what not to say in front of the Queen Mother. Shortly after I started as equerry, I was telling her a story about an Army man and mentioned someone's name. Alastair collared me afterwards and said, 'Let's not name names if there is something negative,' and how right he was.

Another thing Alastair was a master at was letter writing. If I ever wanted to know the correct form of address for a Duke for a letter, I would ask Alastair. He was brilliant. If I had to compare him to anyone, I would say he was similar to Sir Humphrey in *Yes Minister*. He was the king of understatement, but without the edge to him. If there was a problem, the first person I would see was Alastair. If a car had a punctured tyre, you could almost guarantee Ralph's solution would be, 'Ah, well, ah, the Automobile Association will help you. Just ring them and tell them who you are and ask to speak to the chairman.' He just wouldn't have any idea of how to deal with a problem like that, whereas Alastair would say, 'Okay, don't worry about it, just get the Tube and we'll see you when we see you.'

He was a very practical man and a great manager. He knew the many subtleties of the job and the way to handle people perfectly to get the best out of them.

His relationship with the Queen Mother was close, but perhaps not as close as Ralph's. With Alastair there was this air of friendliness and she was obviously very fond of him and trusted him, but there was no real familiarity or chumminess, save for the occasional joke to which everyone in her presence was party. In terms of a social role, this part was played by the ladies-in-waiting. The relationship with Alastair was geared much more around his professional role as private secretary, so she would ask him what was happening at lunch and who had been invited: what would be happening at such and such a place and who would be coming.

Alastair had a much heavier workload than Ralph, whose daily chores could probably have been done in an hour or two. But Ralph's role had changed into more of a social position. If he met a representative from Coutts, he could make a twenty-minute meeting last for half a day with general chit-chat. And as a pair they couldn't have been more different but worked very well as a team, and were often wonderfully funny to watch – heckling each other like the old men in *The Muppet Show*. Whereas Ralph could get angry quite easily, Alastair never saw red. He was always courteous and would laugh off any problems. Without question, the control and overall running of Clarence House was in his hands. Well, actually, it was seventy per cent in his hands and thirty per cent in William's and Reg's, who would often change some aspect of his plans if they didn't like it. And they'd be so subtle in the way they did it. For example, if Alastair had organised a visit to somewhere for lunch or dinner and William and Reg were upset by some part of it, they would feed snippets of information into the Queen Mother's ear at a level no one else could. They would find a way of doing it while she was at her most receptive, perhaps in the evening when she was watching *EastEnders*, and they would just pour it in. They would always hit home. I suppose that's a gift of sorts, though it did cause problems for other members of staff.

Alastair lived in a flat at St James's Palace with his wife, Fiona. She was also employed in the Royal Household and was much more formal in her manner than Alastair ever was. He was quite laid back in his job and even more so outside it. He wore open-necked shirts and cords, totally unlike Ralph. He belonged in the here and now, unlike many of the others.

Ralph and Alastair were the two people I really learned most from during my time there. I remember at one lunch, just after I had arrived, the Queen Mother was offered seconds and said no. As a result, I then said no and Ralph got me afterwards and said, 'You did the right thing there to not accept seconds after the Queen Mother had declined.' It was a matter of politeness. She said no so the rest of her team were expected to say no. When she did encourage you to have seconds, you did. She wasn't a big eater, so she would often just have a nibble before turning to a guest and remarking, 'Oh, you must have some of this.'

But she never asked you directly if you wanted more or if you wanted another drink. That was another point of etiquette that I picked up from Ralph and Alastair. Alastair told me, 'Never ask them if they want more food or another drink, just say things like "Would you like a gin and tonic?" Not "Would you like another?"'

He had picked this up from the Queen Mother and made me aware of it at a very early stage. He also briefed me on things like directional talking, so between him and Ralph they ensured I was never left in the dark.

By far the most down-to-earth member of the home team was the senior lady-in-waiting, Dame Frances Campbell-Preston, who had joined the household in 1965 and was a woman described by Sir Martin Gilliat as 'bringing any form of overt pomposity very quickly to earth'.

She was senior to the five other ladies-in-waiting, who did the job on a two-week rota. Frances was like many senior people at Clarence House in that the further up the chain you were the less pompous you seemed and she had absolutely no airs and graces about her, yet was a superb courtier and knew how to handle people brilliantly. Every evening after finishing at Clarence House she would man a Samaritans hotline. I had no idea she did this until one day I asked her, 'How was your evening, Frances?'

She replied, 'Well, I did an eight-hour shift with the Samaritans last night.'

I, being a bit of a berk, said, 'Really, doing what?' Because I imagined that she made the tea or something.

'Answering phones,' she replied.

You could have knocked me down with a feather duster. I just couldn't believe that a woman so well bred and so high up in the order of things would be doing this. But she was and she was doing a bloody good job by all accounts. She would tell me some heart-wrenching stories and say: 'I had this chap on last night. He was terribly upset. His boyfriend had tried to commit suicide after finding out that most of his heroin had been stolen and this poor chap just didn't know how to handle it. Life's a strange place, isn't it, Colin? But you just have to get on with things.'

I was just blown away that she was putting herself out in such a way to help people much further down the social chain with problems I had never envisaged that she even knew existed. But she did know about them because out of everyone at Clarence House, she was possibly the most streetwise and, although the most senior of the other ladies, she was by far the most down-to-earth. She found working for the Samaritans extremely rewarding and would say to me, 'Some people do have some extraordinary problems.'

She had such a good handle on life. She was the sister-in-law of the comedian and writer Joyce Grenfell, and was able to talk freely with every type of person. I never thought I would go to Clarence House and find out about real life and how to survive it. It was a pleasant surprise. But her life had also been touched by tragedy. While I was there, her granddaughter was eaten by a crocodile during a trip to Africa. She was swimming in a lake and simply disappeared. To this day, her body has never been found. So Frances was well prepared to handle anything that people threw at her and I found her a good point of contact. If I wanted to ask the Queen Mother something that I construed to be a bit delicate or personal – for example, if I wanted the Queen Mother to sign a photo – I would talk to Frances about it.

She occupied almost a kind of chaplain role within the house in terms of counselling and advice and I felt there was nothing she couldn't handle. After all, how many seventy-year-olds do you know who do counselling on a full-time basis? Her role in Clarence House was twenty per cent administration and eighty per cent being a companion to the Queen Mother.

The ladies-in-waiting wrote replies to letters from women's groups and the like and dealt with any personal letters written to the Queen Mother. The rest of the time they acted as her companion and would be on call at all times of the day and night. Their day usually started around 11.00 in the morning, when they would see the Queen Mother and chat to her for a couple of hours before lunch. Later there would be afternoon tea in the lady-in-waiting's office, and whichever lady-in-waiting was on duty would be joined by Alastair, Ralph and me. After that, the lady-in-waiting would spend the evening with the Queen Mother and they would either watch television or chat over a cup of tea. They did have a lot of daily contact with the Queen Mother. But I found that because they only came in for two weeks at a time they never really got into what I called the Clarence House mode, but when they did come in each of them brought a breath of fresh air to the place. They lifted everyone's spirits and seemed like a new face at a time when everybody else could be getting a bit jaded. For example, William and Reg never really took holidays. Their sense of duty made them feel that they never wanted to be seen as taking time off. As they saw it, the Queen Mother never took time off so why should they? They would have weekends on and weekends off, but they were never so far away from Clarence House that they couldn't drop everything and be at the Queen Mother's side in an instant. They always made sure they were within calling distance of Clarence House.

The other companions and ladies-in-waiting included Rachel Bowes Lyon, who wasn't a lady-in-waiting as such, but did the role in an unofficial capacity because she was related to the Queen Mother; Lady Angela Oswald, who was married to Michael Oswald who ran the Queen's stud at Sandringham; and the Honourable Mrs Margaret Rhodes who came from Rhodesia and was one of the famous Rhodes family, and who lived in a cottage in Windsor Great Park. Then there was Jenny Gordon Lennox, who married Captain Gordon Lennox, a Navy officer in charge of the vetting process for military personnel who were going to join the special forces and Elizabeth Bassett, who joined in 1958 and was a quite wonderful woman who collected prayers and collated her own book of prayers. She was probably the kindest human being I have ever met, a woman who cared deeply about people and was selfless in putting others before herself, and whose life had been touched by tragedy when the youngest of her two sons, Peter, shot himself at the age of nineteen, having been bullied in the Army. Others included Jane Walker-Okeover, who ran her own estate at Glenmuick next to Birkhall in Scotland, where she let me stalk on her land; Lady Jean Rankin who had joined in 1947 and who invented the idea of rotating the ladies-in-waiting every two weeks so that the Queen Mother would always have a constant companion to talk to; and Margaret, or Meg, Colville, who was the cheeriest of them all and who had served in the Army with the Queen during the War before being brought into royal duty, where she carved out a niche in alternative medicines, treating ailments such as cuts, bruises, colds, flu and the like with various ointments and creams.

I narrowly missed Ruth Fermoy who was the longest-serving lady-in-waiting and who had been at Clarence House for fifty-seven years. She died shortly before I began working there. By all accounts her death was felt as greatly as that of the late press secretary Martin Gilliat, and Ruth was included on the memorial stone for him in Scotland.

The Queen Mother treated each lady-in-waiting the same and, as far as I could gauge, didn't appear to have a favourite. With the ladies-in-waiting she did unwind a little bit more than she would with the men and was generally more relaxed. The chats were geared more towards women's things and I definitely sensed that the conversations with the ladies-in-waiting were a bit freer of protocol and more open than with the men. All the ladies-in-waiting had their particular strengths. I don't think I could put my finger on any weaknesses and they were very easy people to work with, apart from one instance at Birkhall when I was discussing the following day's plans with Jenny and she said, 'The Stairs are coming down tomorrow.'

'What do you mean "coming down"?' I said, 'Why have you only told me this now? I mean, what sort of arrangements are we going to make for the Queen Mother?' I was suddenly rather worried.

She looked at me as if I were completely bonkers: 'The usual arrangements apply for receiving guests.'

'Receiving guests?' I said. 'How can we receive guests with building work going on? What are we going to do with them, and more to the point, where is the Queen Mother going to sleep?'

'What are you talking about?' she added.

'The stairs, you said the stairs are coming down.' My eyes at this point were straining to burst out of their sockets.

She laughed, 'Lord and Lady Stair are coming.'

I slumped back in my seat: 'Oh, thank God for that,' I said. 'Oh, thank you. That won't be a problem. Blimey, I thought builders were going to arrive any minute.'

The loyalty all staff had towards the Queen Mother could be gauged whenever they were ill. All the Clarence House staff were ill at some point when I was there, either they would have a bad cold or flu or in some cases something much worse, but the funny thing was they just wouldn't stop working. People would come in with the most appalling ailments and I had to say to them, 'Look, just go away, go home. Just don't come to work in that state.'

There were other things to consider as well. Employees would have too much to drink the night before and they'd come in with the most dreadful hangovers. But by far the biggest problem was dealing with staff fallouts. You'd have butlers falling out with kitchen staff all the time and this would cause massive tension. I'd often hear raised voices behind stairs. My one big fallout was with William over a painting that needed to be collected from a shop in London. I wasn't there to collect it because I was in Scotland looking after the Queen Mother's affairs at Birkhall. So no one took responsibility for it and I got this curt phone call from William, who could easily have stepped in and collected it on my behalf. Instead, he tried to torpedo me. He said, 'Look, there's no one here to collect this painting because we're all far too busy.'

I just couldn't believe that was the case and said, 'Couldn't you just find half an hour out of your day to go and collect it, or send one of the footmen to get it?'

'No,' was his blunt response.

'Fine,' I said, and it didn't get collected.

On my return, I was furious and took him to one side and said, 'Look, the fact that this painting hasn't been collected doesn't make me look bad, it makes the Queen Mother look bad. There was an arrangement with the shop for it to be collected and it looks like she's let them down, so I suggest a bit more co-operation between you and me will help her tremendously.'

I had learned the valuable rules of the game, to make this not about me but the Queen Mother. We both knew it and it didn't need to be said. We never had a cross word after that.

CHAPTER SIX

'HAVE I DIED AGAIN?'

After a few months in the job my relationship with the Queen Mother was blossoming. She had started to open up towards me and seemed a little more relaxed when I was getting on with things, confident that I knew what I was doing. We would often have a laugh and a joke but, more importantly, I had established a good professional working relationship with her. My role was slightly different as well. I was the first one of her many equerries to take on a much wider brief that incorporated some of the media duties undertaken by her late press secretary Sir Martin Gilliat, who wasn't replaced when he died. So the equerry's job suddenly became much more complex, though not an adrenalin rush by any stretch of the imagination. One of my additional roles was to go to ITV every now and then to check that they had got their facts right for the Queen

Mother's obituary, which they had ready to run in case of any eventuality. They had put together a number of different scenarios for her death, including ones at Royal Lodge, the Castle of Mey, Windsor and Birkhall, to name but a few. My job was to sit and watch these with a team and say: 'Yes, that chap there is Alastair Aird… Yes, there's William Tallon… Yes, that's Birkhall,' and so forth, basically reviewing it for them.

It was odd to be lunching with the Queen Mother one minute and then watching details of her death the next, before seeing her alive and well again the following day. But there were hiccups. Most media organisations had something prepared in case she died suddenly. In 1993, a Sky TV employee caught sight of such a rehearsal and, thinking it was a real broadcast, leaked it through his mother to the Australian media, which then put out premature reports of her death. A couple of years later, it happened again, when a newspaper wrongly reported her demise. This somehow made its way back to the Queen Mother, probably through one of the butlers, and she came into the room where we were all gathered ready for lunch and said, 'Oh, I see I'm dead again!'

She just thought it was so hilarious and added, 'They are such silly people.'

Reviewing her obituary, it was interesting to see how these programmes were done. When Diana died in 1997, it was rather spooky to see how the BBC got everything together and in place so quickly in terms of facts, interviews and library footage. But of course, they had prepared this information months, if not years, in advance. I never told the

Queen Mother about the obituary reviews, which I reviewed twice. But if I had, I'm sure she would have appreciated the irony of it and probably would have repeated her 'I'm dead again' comment.

Fortunately, one thing the extra responsibility did get me was a promotion in rank. Previous equerries were all required to hold at least the rank of captain. But with the extra responsibility, they upgraded the job to the rank of major, although it was only as an acting rank which meant they could take it off you when you left that role. At the junior staff college, prior to arriving at Clarence House, I had galloped into my promotional exams with all the gusto of someone who was going to fly helicopters in Australia if it didn't work out. Needless to say, I was a little distracted and barely scraped through without being shot. But all that changed when I was given the position as the Queen Mother's equerry, which meant that I was promoted to major immediately. I was twenty-six years old and suddenly became one of the youngest majors in the Army and, when I finished my two years with the Queen Mother, I was allowed to keep the rank, which was a good moment for me, and for my father. It wasn't a bad achievement for one so young.

Another good moment was when I left the household and was made an MVO, which stands for Member of the Victorian Order, and attended an investiture at Buckingham Palace. It is a reasonably senior order and higher than an MBE. It was created by Queen Victoria and is given almost exclusively at the discretion of the Royal Family, as opposed to other orders, such as OBEs, MBEs and such, where the government of the day draws up a list and it is up to the Monarch to ratify it. So I was quite pleased to get this. At the time, my job was the shortest job in history that resulted in such an honour. It took people like Phil Collins ten years of Royal Variety Performances and more to get theirs, and, at that time, in the mid nineties, only a couple of thousand had ever been issued. I remember feeling quite proud when I turned up at Buckingham Palace to receive it. The Queen pinned it on my chest and said, 'That wasn't too hard, was it?' and we both smiled at each other because she and I knew that people climbed Everest to get one of these, and here I was, a mere equerry, part of the furniture, being awarded one of the most prestigious orders there is. It is a good thing to have, though I never really use it, but there was one occasion at a media event, where a rather pompous woman made much of her MBE. I replied, 'It's always good to meet members of junior orders.' Some meaningful stares ensued but after enquiring about the Victorian Order, she gave me a wry smile and continued circulating.

The role of equerry was a comfortable one, quite easy and very enlightening. Clarence House was a fairly sedate place, quite straightforward and quiet. Given the Queen Mother's age, the number of her engagements had been dramatically reduced and were relatively low-key in tone, although while I was there, she was the royal representative chosen to decommission the British Aircraft Carrier *Ark Royal* temporarily prior to its receiving a massive refurbishment. Apart from that, there was nothing very remarkable that she attended and most of her week, when not at Scotland, was spent at Clarence House. I found that I had quite a bit of down time. The Queen Mother didn't really entertain in the evenings, so I had those to myself, and during the day the whole atmosphere of the place was very calm. But it was important that I got things right because mistakes were not always that easy to cover up. You couldn't forget to book a helicopter, or something like that. If you had a bank of photographers waiting for the Queen Mother's helicopter to take off from Norfolk and you had forgotten to book the chopper, it wasn't something that could be quickly set right. Any mistakes seemed much bigger, mainly because they would be played out very publicly with the world's media looking on.

I did make mistakes, although I don't think I dropped any real humdingers. I remember one televised occasion when I turned up wearing the wrong uniform. I had the wrong belt on. It really wasn't that obvious to anyone, apart from a particularly keen-eyed retired colonel who was watching the whole thing on television and spotted me wearing the wrong accessories and rang Alastair to tell him. Alastair had to hang on the line while this bumptious old boy with nothing better to do rambled on about it. It was left to Alastair to have a quiet word with me. He simply said, 'Try to get it right next time, eh? Makes my life a lot easier. Still, I didn't even notice it myself. There you go.'

A similar sort of thing happened to an officer who was invited to dinner at Windsor Castle. He was there to meet the Royal Family at Christmas. It was probably the most important dinner party invitation he would ever receive in his life. He turned up in his mess kit, which is all red with a black tie. It's rather like an old British Rail outfit. In fact, if he'd walked down a train wearing it, people would have asked him for a coffee. During the evening at the castle, as the Royal Family mingled with the guests, the Queen said to him, 'Aren't you supposed to be wearing a stiff wing collar?' To which he replied, 'Oh yes, we do sometimes, but only on very special occasions.'

It was true: the members of his regiment only wore wing collars on very special occasions, but what could be more special than dinner with the Royal Family? But the poor guy was so nervous that the last thing he had thought about was a wing collar. Suffice it to say, he went a deep crimson, as red as the suit he was wearing, and the Queen just smiled and said, 'Well, maybe you'll wear it for the next special occasion.'

Meeting royalty like that does faze a lot of people, but for my part, I felt when I was picked for the job of equerry that the Queen Mother must have been comfortable with me doing the job; this knowledge gave me the confidence to relax and from then on I didn't really worry much about it after that. It was a good moment in my career because I felt that, unlike most jobs, this one hinged on your personality. It wasn't very stressful, and before I knew it I was spending time and having conversations with the Queen Mother that people far senior to me could never have scheduled. She would ask me what I did on my weekends off, where I went for dinner, or if I met any girls.

'Did you get lucky?' she would ask.

I didn't suppose for a moment that our respective definitions of 'getting lucky' were remotely the same, though.

I remember when I was only a few weeks into the job and I took a girl from the South African Embassy out for dinner and the Queen Mother's eyes lit up at hearing this and she said, 'Oh, fast work! I am impressed!' She loved the courtship rituals of young people. I think it took her back to her youth.

About two months into my handover, I got the measure of the job and knew I could handle most things quite competently. Occasionally, I would be taken by surprise and think, what do I do here, but that happened right up to the end of my tenure. Situations such as meeting Lord Slim and him punching me in the stomach were something that I just wasn't prepared for. But really it was the finer details you had to be wary of. The big things tended to look after themselves. And the Queen Mother wasn't an unreasonable person to work for; in fact, to this day, I don't think I have worked for anybody who was more reasonable. Most of her requests started with 'Is there any chance you could do this?' or 'If it's not too much trouble, could you bring this?' Of course, any member of staff would drop everything to do her bidding. The weird thing about it was that the more involvement you had with the Queen Mother, the easier the whole process was in a way. It was better to be close to her than distant from her.

One thing I was aware of was her supposed iron will, described wonderfully by the writer and historian Sir Roy Strong, who was a regular lunch guest, when he wrote, 'The

Queen Mother's beguiling mask of humorous charm was belied by the determined set of the lips.'

This iron will could manifest itself in quite brutal ways. When Edward VIII acceded to the throne in 1936, the Queen Mother and her husband, Albert – then the Duke and Duchess of York – were invited to Balmoral for dinner with Edward's future wife, Wallis Simpson, acting as hostess. As soon as the Queen Mother walked in, she went past Wallis blasting, 'I have come to dine with the King,' and sat to the right of him throughout proceedings as usual.

I looked for this streak of steel in her but, by 1994, I think she was generally a bit calmer. There was definitely a warmth about her, though, and it was nothing to do with what she said or did; she was just quite thoughtful. If I were ever working late, she would say to me, 'I do hope you don't need to be somewhere else.'

The only time the warmth was dropped was in matters of protocol. If protocol wasn't adhered to, she could get quite firm and often did with the butlers. The only time she was ever really testy with me in terms of overstepping the boundary was when we were at Royal Lodge in Windsor Great Park. Some guests arrived and I decided to put their coats in a nearby closet. Suddenly, I heard a stern voice say, 'Oh, no, don't go in there. It's a very secret place.'

I turned round and there was the Queen Mother smiling, but behind the smile was this narrow-eyed determination that I should do as she said and obviously I did.

It wasn't the worst moment of my two years there. The lowest point came during her annual trip to Royal Ascot.

The Queen Mother went in a police-escorted limousine. I went in my own car. But I hadn't banked on the horrendous traffic which parted for the Queen Mother's car, but not for me. So I turned up thirty minutes late and the first person I saw was Ralph, who, red-faced, said to me, 'You're late!'

The Queen Mother wasn't really bothered, but I could tell some of her staff were. It really wasn't a good moment and I was about to say to Ralph that I hadn't got the luxury of a police escort, but then thought better of it. It got worse a few weeks later when I was at a drinks party at Royal Lodge and bumped into Alastair's wife, Fiona. She came up to me and said, 'Oh, you're here. I thought you would be late again.'

I felt like I had been punched in the face, it was a petty thing to say. But that's the problem with working there. It was a great job but there was no margin for error and when you made a mistake, boy did people remember it.

Generally, the morale of the place was high mainly because everybody enjoyed working for the Queen Mother. As an employer, she never said, 'You have done a good job there.' It just wasn't her thing and it was rather expected of you to do a good job anyway. But she would sometimes say things such as 'That was a lovely meal, thank you very much,' and you could see how it lifted the staff.

She really seemed to care about other people's feelings and tempered her decision-making to how her staff would be able to cope with it, which was very magnanimous of her. She wasn't constrained by the sort of ceremonial duties other Royals had to perform – even though she took her duties very seriously indeed – so she could if she so wished wake up one morning and decide she wanted to go to Scotland or go on holiday and she could do this completely on a whim and nobody could stop her. But this never happened because she knew it would cause severe disruption to the household. Instead, we stuck to the itinerary and a routine which made it a lot easier for everyone. She was also very aware of the importance, especially during visits, that people placed on her in terms of what they were hoping for when they met her. For instance, a good trick I saw her use was to stop in the middle of a line-up and say to someone: 'How is your brother getting on?' Obviously, she had been briefed that this person had a brother, and their mouth would open in amazement.

She had this ability to leave you bursting with pride and completely overwhelmed after just a few words or by some little act that she had done on your behalf. She did this to me when I was leaving after my two years as equerry. I had a farewell meeting with her in her study and when I entered the room she was sitting at a desk scribbling away on something that looked like a Post-it note. I thought, what's going on here then? She gave me this small piece of paper and said, 'I have been reading some of Winston Churchill's speeches and thought this would be a nice thing to take away with you.'

I looked down at the Post-it and she had written on it: 'Never Flinch, Never Weary, Never Despair.'

It was Churchill's wartime battle cry and summed up her whole attitude to life. When the Royal Family was in crisis during the abdication in the thirties and the marriage difficulties of the younger royals in the nineties, she was the one who remained calm. She ploughed on regardless and her view of every moment of those turmoils was that she could get through it by maintaining this air of stoicism. Those words on that little bit of paper reflected all that she had been through over the years and I was touched. I also received the mandatory cufflinks as a leaving present, as every equerry does. They have her initials engraved on one side and you put your initials on the other. But I wasn't expecting the note. It knocked me for six. All I could think was that this lady had taken the time to go to her study, look up Churchill's speeches, find something she thought was appropriate and write it down. I almost ended up in tears. Out of all the things I got, and I received photographs and books from people like Ted Hughes and stored up some glorious memories, that note from the Queen Mother is the one thing I will really treasure forever.

The hardest part of the job was the fact that there was no clear road map for what I was doing, but in a way, it was also the most rewarding. I found I just had to react to what went on around me day by day and, even though one had to stick to protocol, basically every situation was new. Sometimes I would meet an artist, other times a general. One day, I would be delivering flowers to one of the Queen Mother's friends in hospital, another, I might be by her side on a royal walkabout. It could be stressful, but in another way it was stimulating to be in a job where every single day was different. I had to make sure that every aspect of the Queen Mother's life was happy and pleasant and that the good times far, far outweighed the bad. And what was really enjoyable was when things went a bit off track. For example, if we had a plan for the day and at the last minute the Queen Mother decided she wanted to do something a little bit different, that could be quite fun. In fact, it was brilliant because there was spontaneity there. The whole nature of the job was so far removed from working for a company like ICI or Ford where your loyalty was to the company. At Clarence House everyone concentrated on one person, the Queen Mother. We could tell when she was having fun and enjoying herself because at those times well-laid plans tended to go out of the window. She would say something like, 'Oh, let's not have lunch at Clarence House today, let's go to Claridges,' or on a company visit she might say: 'I'm sure it would be quicker this way,' and the private secretary would be muttering to himself, 'Oh no, oh no.'

The difficult thing was remembering the numerous rules of etiquette and this applied especially to people meeting the Queen Mother for the first time. In most jobs there are no rules as to what to say or do when meeting the managing director or chairman of a company; you are just generally expected to be polite. However, in the military, the most minor soldier knows how to address a major because the Army, as with royalty, is run on strict ground rules. People who met the Queen Mother for the first time would sometimes be in a bit of a panic and ask me, 'What do I do, what do I do?'

I would then explain the few simple rules to follow when in the presence of a member of the Royal Family. I would tell them that at the first instance you had to address her as 'Your Majesty' and bow, and if you left the room you should bow again to her before leaving, unless you were going in and out all the time. For me, it was more a token gesture to nod my head to her if I left the room. Once you had called her 'Your Majesty', you would say 'ma'am' after that. By the way, 'ma'am' is pronounced like 'jam'; people who stretch out the middle 'a' because they think they are being posh are a source of great amusement to the Royal Family. There weren't that many rules to follow and once I had explained this to people and they realised that there were only one or two things to remember, they felt much more at ease. Some people came to Clarence House for lunch visibly shaking, they would be so worried. But I would do my best to reassure them; sometimes, I even had to show women how to curtsey properly, and you can only imagine how that must have looked! I would say, 'It's really easy. Just remember only to shake hands with her if she offers a hand. Don't speak unless you're spoken to and don't talk over her. That's it really.'

But the Queen Mother was so accomplished socially that she could make any guest feel at ease within seconds. I have had more stressful dinner parties outside Clarence House than inside.

CHAPTER SEVEN

'OH, BLOODY HELL!'

It was August 1995, and the Queen Mother was at Birkhall for her annual summer break. I was the first down for breakfast; it was the done thing for the equerry to be first down because he was the Queen Mother's representative if she were absent – in any case, the Queen Mother always had breakfast in her room. So while she was upstairs, I would be downstairs making sure that all the other guests were being fed and were generally okay. On this particular occasion, as I was tucking into my cereal, I happened to glance at the *Daily Mirror* and saw a front-page exclusive screaming out yet more embarrassing revelations about Prince Charles. Now estranged from Diana, he was having a tough time. She was feeding all sorts of stories to the press, and the 'Camillagate' nonsense had almost destroyed his credibility. Prince Charles was at Birkhall for the week. He had effectively come up to escape all this and do a bit of sketching in the hills. Now there was this. I looked at it with mounting panic because Charles could come in at any moment. So I hid it at the bottom of the newspaper pile and made sure the *Times*, *Daily Telegraph*, *Independent* and all the others were on top. Sure enough, minutes later, in he came. There were just the two of us in the room. I wanted to shrink into my chair and disappear. I was almost willing him not to pick up the papers and silently saying, don't do it, please don't do it, but he did, and he started going through them one by one and just looking at the front page. Then he got to the *Mirror*. Suddenly, his face contorted into this pained and hurt expression and he cried, 'Oh, bloody hell, these bloody people! Why don't they just leave me a-bloody-lone?'

I didn't know how to handle this situation. Prince Charles never really took himself that seriously, so as he read the offending report he shouted, 'What the bloody hell, oh, what the bloody hell,' before reading the next paragraph which would make him laugh because he found the whole thing utterly ridiculous. Then he'd get annoyed again at the next paragraph and shout, 'These people. How dare they say this about me,' and he would slam his fists on the table.

As he did this, I just sat there quietly horrified as my cereal bowl jolted up and down. I tried to look as sympathetic as possible, especially when he kept turning to me and saying, 'Look at them, look at them,' and pointing at the paper.

I wanted to say something, to come out in sympathy, but what the hell could I say? What would anyone say in this

Top left: Attending the Queen Mother's birthday celebrations in 1995.

©*Michael Jones*

Top right: The Queen Mother shows off her falconry skills at Birkhall.

Above: A view of Sandringham from across the lake.

Right: Outside the Polver fishing cabin at Birkhall.

Ranger relaxes under a footstall.

Catriona Leslie and Sir Ralph Anstruther listen to *The Archers* at Birkhall.

Birkhall in summer bloom.

Rush, Minnie and Ranger wait for a sausage at the end of a picnic lunch.

In search of grouse with the Hon. Edward Dawson-Damer, Captain Ashe Wyndham and the Hon. Phillip Astor.

The Royal Wessex Helicopter.

Highland cattle at Birkhall. They taste as good as they look.

The Queen Mother stops for a cup of tea with a retired worker on the Balmoral estate.

Top left: A dinner guest in Saddam Hussein mask chats to an unruffled Queen Mother after dinner.

Top right: The kitchen staff at Birkhall.

Above: A good spot for salmon fishing at Birkhall.

Right: The culmination of a day's deer hunting.

Top left: The Castle of Mey in glorious sunshine.

Top right: Ranger, Rush and Minnie wait outside the Queen Mother's room.

Above: A picnic lunch at Caithness.

Left: With the first salmon I caught at Birkhall.

The Queen Mother makes a joke about how much I've brought to drink.

On the Balmoral estate in 1995.

Corgi chaos.

At parties, men hope to be dressed alike, whereas this is ladies' greatest concern. A winning combination here.

The Queen Mother with David Linley.

Preparing for a picnic lunch at Sandringham.

Leaving church at Caithness.

William Tallon helps Ranger down from the BAE 146.

Top: Birkhall.

Bottom left: The Queen Mother arrives at Caithness on her flight from London.

Bottom right: The corgis finish up the sausages.

type of situation? I got on with my breakfast quietly. I thought it best to say nothing at all and just let him ride it out. He wasn't embarrassed by these revelations at all. He was simply very angry and extremely annoyed that someone was reporting on his life in so intrusive a way. But that is the big contradiction in being royal, your life isn't really your own. In reality, you belong to the public, who through taxes pay for your upkeep, and to a point Charles recognised this. But in 1995, the trickle of news stories had become a flood and most of them were anti-Charles and pro-Diana. He was having problems coming to terms with this and wanted the whole of the media to cut him some slack and get off his back. Unfortunately for him, he had a vengeful wife who was determined to stick the knife in at every available opportunity. At that time, Charles and Camilla were still meant to be a secret, albeit a very bad one, and the only thing the Clarence House staff picked up on was what was in the papers, and much of that was hearsay. So that relationship wasn't really discussed in the household. But it was interesting to go in each day and hear about any new revelations that had broken, some of which would be read with open mouths by Alastair and Ralph, who couldn't believe what was going on.

Prince Charles sought solace with the Queen Mother during these horrendous years. He was by far and away her favourite grandchild and one whom she would see regularly, at least two or three times a week. She was his escape route and the person he confided in more than anyone else, and these chats were closed meetings. None of the staff was ever privy to them. The Queen Mother had a simple way of dealing with the Charles and Diana problem if ever a staff member or guest tried to bring up the subject – at that time they were on the verge of divorce proceedings and were the most talked about couple on earth, and I think at least half a dozen people, including me, dare to mention them. She would greet the question with a simple: 'Some things are better left unsaid.'

It was quite clear that she had no love at all for Diana but all the time in the world for Charles. And it was becoming more apparent by the day that the Princess of Wales was, let's say, complex, both outwardly and inwardly. She had a very complicated family and had her own personal issues to deal with. If you mix all this with her involvement with the Royal Family, it was an unfortunate recipe and through her marriage to Charles she had found herself transported from the modern world into a very old-fashioned one with certain ways of doing things. It's something you either bend to or you don't. She had found it a huge adjustment to act as the traditional consort of the heir to the throne and, with the media spotlight on her, it all became a bit too intense and she couldn't cope. In this respect, she never visited Clarence House while I was there. She kept to her apartments in Kensington Palace, having her affairs and making crank telephone calls, and as far as the Queen Mother was concerned she was very much *persona non grata* because her name was never brought up by, or in front of, the Queen Mother. But this was in stark contrast to Charles. Their relationship was very close. Although, while he was her favourite, Charles was run a close second by Princess

Margaret's son Viscount Linley. But Charles and the Queen Mother shared a set of old-fashioned values and he, like her, wanted to make people feel comfortable and at ease.

Charles' private persona is far removed from the public view of him as the bumbling man endlessly going on about architecture and talking to plants. When you meet him, as I discovered almost as soon as I started at Clarence House, you find that he is incredibly charming, engaging and funny. One of his party pieces, which he still does to this day, so I'm told, came about when a visit by the Queen Mother had been planned to a German town in the 1970s. The Germans had invited her to stay with a local dignitary and they sent over an itinerary for the trip, as was usual for most visits and tours. But because they wanted to do things properly and show just how efficient they could be, the agenda, lined up for the full five days she was there, had been planned down to the exact minute. They had written that breakfast would be served at such and such a time and finished by X time and then at Y time they would do this and finish at Z time. Of course, it was typical of German efficiency but it was so detailed and so planned that Charles kept the itinerary and from time to time he got it out in the drawing room at Birkhall and, in a ridiculous comic German accent, he would say, 'Unt at svive of ze clock, ve vill be going parascending unt ze lady-in-waiting vill be going schuba divink. You vill den go to zee glass factory unt ze lady-in-waiting vill have ze chance to blow ze glass bubbles.' And he would rip through this while I was having pre-dinner drinks with guests simply having a laugh. The only thing he didn't do was start goose-stepping.

Added to this wicked streak of humour is his intelligence. Charles is extremely intelligent and very knowledgeable. When he was on his regular visits to Clarence House, he would always find time to talk various members of staff and I had lots of conversations with him about things as diverse as the state of the world and the Queen Mother's state of health. He would often pop in and the first thing he would ask me would be, 'So, how is my grandmother? Is she still feeling fit and healthy? Is she in a good mood today?' His love for her can best be summed up not in what he said to me but in one of his most famous quotes in a speech in which he said,

Ever since I can remember, my grandmother has been a most wonderful example of fun, laughter and, above all, exquisite taste in so many things. For me she has always been one of those extraordinary rare people whose touch can turn everything to gold. She belongs to that priceless band of human beings whose greatest gift is to enhance life for others through their own effervescent enthusiasm for life.

It was the Queen Mother who interested Charles in homoeopathic medicine. She was very keen on alternative treatments and I remember coming in with a bruise on my arm one day and she gave me a bottle of cream that you would never find at a chemist for me to rub on it. I still have the bottle with her seal on it. She was very keen on these herbal remedies and gave me lots of things like that so I can fully understand why Prince Charles was influenced by her.

If your grandmother is nearly 100 years old and says to you, this is how I like to keep healthy, then you're going to listen to her rather than some fifty-year-old doctor, and Charles constantly took her advice and acted on it.

Above all, Charles was incredibly polite and nice in the way he addressed people. He would never be rude, except to some members of his own staff, which I will talk of later. Generally, he was just very gentle and quite calm. He was a typical example of a gentleman, as in a 'gentle man'. Add to this his self-deprecating nature and you have a pretty potent mix. He really could charm the socks of virtually everyone he met. And this calm, polite and very pleasant character was far removed from the public's perception of him. I saw people who met him be totally absorbed by his whole character and personality. Others recognised him from the television news and photographs and felt as if they knew him intimately and that he almost belonged to them, in the same way that people do about celebrities when they see them constantly on television. One of his best traits was his storytelling, most of which was against himself. I remember one story he told me, one of his favourites, in which he said, 'Colin, people don't like characters who fudge around the issues and I like people who come straight to the point.' He added:

My groundskeeper was getting rid of some of the heather once from some Birkhall land and I had just planted thousands of young saplings in this area. So my groundsman goes out and gets rid of the heather and when he'd finished just comes straight up to me in my office and says, 'Your Royal Highness, you know those saplings you planted?' and I said, 'Yes.' 'Well, I've burnt the bloody lot!'

'And I was just so shocked. I couldn't be angry, because he hadn't given me any time to be angry. Instead, he'd been so upfront about it and so aggressive in the way he said it that I just could not be annoyed with him. I just told him, 'Oh, okay, well, erm, what happened then?' and he explained and that was that.

Although this was one conflict Charles could easily resolve there were others that he found rather more difficult. He often clashed with his staff and his advisors.

He always got experts in to deal with matters surrounding his various businesses. For instance, he asked people from Crabtree & Evelyn in to set up his Highgrove shop which sold organic produce, and he sought advice from an ex-John Lewis senior manager, David Stevens, on how to run it. He would work very closely with all his advisors, inviting them for lunches and dinners, until before they knew it they had become totally wrapped up in his life and began to misread their level of involvement in it. Eventually, of course, they would stray from their brief and begin advising on other matters and ask him about his marriage problems or his relationship with Camilla, and the moment they started to do that, he got rid of them. As quickly as they came they would be gone. It happened with his staff, too. Charles comes from a family whose members are used to getting whatever they want when they want. So towards the end of the twentieth century, when new employment laws were introduced that effectively meant you couldn't get rid of employees willy-nilly if there were a problem with them, there was an immediate problem, because in Charles' mind he could get rid of whomsoever he bloody well pleased. Prince Charles didn't want to know that if there were a chauffeur he didn't like and wanted to get rid of, he had to give him a verbal warning followed by two written warnings before he could sack him. He would simply say: 'Why should I do this, just get rid of him.'

He thought the employment laws were crazy. If he didn't like someone he thought it his natural right to get rid of him or her, especially if the person weren't up to the job, and he did get rid of them, leaving his personnel officer to pick up the pieces. They had to be paid off, sometimes with huge amounts of money. I know chauffeurs who walked out of his employ with upwards of £50,000. It was a ridiculous situation. I was lucky in so many ways. My job was far less formal than that of Charles' equerry. He had to wear a uniform much more often than I did and conduct himself in a very formal and businesslike manner throughout the working day, the routine was strictly observed. And he didn't get to sit down with Charles every day and enjoy lunch with him. It was as far removed from my role as it could possibly be.

The only other conflicts that arose came when Prince Charles tried to speak his mind. As far as he is concerned, he can pretty much say whatever he pleases. I remember occasions when remarks of his would be blown completely out of proportion in the press and he would look at me with despair in his eyes and say, 'But I'm only voicing an opinion.'

When the government of the day took the official line on things, he liked to give an alternative viewpoint. He thought it the role of the Royal Family to question the status quo and what was going on in society. He is much more lef-wing than the Queen Mother and politically he does swing very much towards New Labour. He would have made an excellent secretary of state for culture. He believes that the Royal Family isn't here simply for entertainment value; he sees them playing a major part in people's lives, and he enjoys taking a line that to some seems quite controversial, especially on things like architecture, because he believes it sparks a debate in the country as a whole and gets people involved in something. He is also aware that he isn't getting any younger and the prospect of him becoming king seems remote so he wants to make an impact and carve a niche for himself as a spokesperson for traditional values and a decent way of life.

He has always tried to do the right thing, and coming from a family whose historical values made this paramount, he didn't really have much choice. Doing the right thing is almost the Royal Family's motto because they know that if this isn't adhered to the whole concept of the British Monarchy could tumble down around their ears. For example, if you look back at Edward abdicating because he wanted to marry Wallis Simpson, he didn't do what he wanted to do, which was to marry her and still be king. He had to do what his family and the government believed was right at the time and abdicate. Two options were open to him: to marry her and abdicate, or not to marry and still be king. He chose the former. Similarly, Henry VIII changed the whole religious framework of the country for his own purposes. Another good example is Princess Margaret, who didn't marry the one love of her life, Captain Peter Townsend. She wanted to be seen to be doing right, but it broke her heart.

Charles married Diana because he saw it as the right thing to do, even if there was no real love between them, especially on his part. If you have spent time with Charles, as I have, you will realise that they just weren't suited to each other. But she came from the right background. She was young and attractive and it was seen as a fairytale wedding when Charles married this perfect, almost shy and somewhat coquettish young woman. But when it all went wrong, Charles realised that the true love of his life was Camilla, who, like him, shared his love of a quieter, more old-fashioned lifestyle. At some stage, probably a couple of years after Diana's death, he must have looked at the abdication of Edward and the way Margaret gave up the love of her life and considered very carefully the balance between his personal relationship and public. In a way this undermines the decisions of his ancestors. Perhaps this influenced why he waited until his grandmother had died before committing himself. She would never have approved. But it has finally brought him happiness after years of despair, worry and stress. It is fair to say that his life has been touched by tragedy; the failure of his marriage and the death of Diana, are but two examples.

But the most upset I ever saw Charles had nothing to do

with his marriage or anything connected to it; it was when he lost his dog Pooh. We were at Birkhall and Charles had gone walking with Pooh, his Jack Russell, when the dog just disappeared. He had clearly gone down a rabbit hole and got stuck, but Charles didn't know where – or how – he had managed to do this, and he was never found. Well, Charles was absolutely beside himself with grief. He spent all that night with a torch looking for him together with me and as many of the Birkhall staff as he could lay his hands on. It was one of those times where we all thought, oh, we'll find him eventually. But as five minutes turned to ten, and ten to twenty, there was a dawning realisation that Pooh had gone. Eventually Charles said to me, eyes red from tears: 'Look, you go on back and take the staff with you. I'm going to carry on the search alone.'

He stayed out there all night, desperately looking for his dog and digging around on his hands trying to find the rabbit hole that he had gone down. But as dawn broke, he gave up and came back inside, and for most of the next day you could see him occasionally about to well up. He would suddenly become distant as he thought of his dog trapped in a hole, slowly starving to death. It was very hard for him to take, and although he and the Queen Mother were close, she didn't really console him. You have to bear in mind that all her friends and most of her family had died, so a dog didn't really register with her. I just remember her saying to him when he told her what had happened: 'Oh, I'm sorry to hear that. Anyway, have some tea.'

It took him years to get over the loss of that dog.

CHAPTER EIGHT

THE RELUCTANT ROYAL AND A MAN IN A HURRY

The Queen Mother would always talk in the very fondest terms about all her grandchildren and would never put any of them down, well, not to members of her staff anyway. But the years 1994 to 1996 were ones of deep worry for her. She worried about all of them, especially Prince Andrew whom she thought had been treated quite badly by Sarah Ferguson. At the time, Andrew and Fergie, as everyone thought of her, had split up, but they kept seeing each other on and off for ages afterwards and I remember the Queen Mother sighing and saying to me, 'You know Andrew does love her so.'

And you could see that in spite of everything Sarah Ferguson had done, in spite of all the shame she had brought on the Royals with her affairs and her gaffes, the Queen Mother was still quite fond of her because of the joy she brought to Andrew. In the Queen Mother's eyes, if you were happy with someone, it didn't really matter about anything else, just so long as that love and happiness prevailed. But Andrew wasn't happy. He felt life had dealt him a bad hand compared to Charles and to compensate he threw himself into work and was like a man in a hurry, always rushing about. As a consequence, he never really relaxed and could get quite angry with the people around him. During my time at Clarence House, he had quite a vigorous military schedule. He had been a pilot and a navy officer and ended up running a Royal Navy air force base, which was quite a senior position within the armed forces. This gave him a totally different persona to that of Prince Charles who was a very artistic and philosophical kind of person. Andrew, on the other hand, was very black and white about things; there was a wrong way and a right way and that was that. You could see the difference in the way they viewed the Queen Mother's staff. Charles viewed the Queen Mother's household as her companions, whereas Andrew perceived the staff as mere employees who were to be treated as such. Charles saw my role as more of a social one, while Andrew saw me as the Queen Mother's equerry who organised trips and oversaw various aspects of her correspondence and that was that. I saw Andrew about once a month, when he came to visit Clarence House, and he would talk to the staff, including me, as an officer talks to his subordinates. He would say things such as: 'I want this done and I want it done now' or 'Have that done by such and such a time'.

I remember him always saying 'Do it!' which was his catchphrase of sorts. The Queen Mother's household just put up with his brusqueness. Where it did cause problems was among his own staff. I remember his equerry, Rupert Maitland-Titterton, falling out with him seriously when Andrew was going to take a train to Birmingham. It wasn't a royal train, just a regular service train. Rupert's job was to make sure that Andrew arrived fifteen minutes before the departure time and that he got on safely. Poor old Rupert went rushing ahead only to discover that the train to Birmingham had been cancelled. The stationmaster told him that the Duke of York could wait in the VIP lounge until the next train was ready to leave (I think they were every hour). Well, of course, when Andrew arrived, he was fuming about the train being cancelled and he vented his rage on Rupert, at one point screaming at him, 'Why can't they organise another train?' He then flicked his hand and shouted, 'That train over there, for example, why can't they divert that train to Birmingham?'

Rupert was desperately trying to come up with the answers but couldn't, and in the end he lost it and retorted, 'Look, do I have a British Rail badge on my lapel? No, I don't, because I don't bloody well work for British Rail.' And the more he spoke the angrier he got, and he ended up shouting at the prince: 'If you want to talk about bloody trains, talk to the bloody stationmaster. I'm the equerry, and I'm trying to do the best I can do to make your life as comfortable as possible.'

I don't think Prince Andrew had ever been spoken to by

a member of staff like that in his life. He was so taken aback at being stood up to in such a forthright manner that he ended up saying to him, 'Okay, fine, let's just wait and see what they can do.'

Of course, Andrew had the frustration of having to take public transport because there was a clash in his status of being a Royal and yet not so senior that a royal train would be commissioned for him. That was because, by accident of birth, by being the Queen's second son, he was classed as a minor Royal. It irritated him. He didn't like to feel second class. The royal pecking order didn't sit comfortably with him. He saw himself as a military officer, as a war veteran who had done a lot for his country, including risking his life in combat, and as an ambassador for his nation, rather than as an armchair Royal who sits on the trappings of power and wealth without actually ever doing anything. So to deny him the luxuries of royalty seemed a bit petty in his eyes and this tended to cloud his general outlook on life. Whenever he came to visit the Queen Mother, he was never really chatty like Prince Charles and, unlike his elder brother, showed absolutely no interest in the staff and their personal lives. In all honesty, he wasn't a particularly nice person. I remember nearly telling him where to go when he came into Clarence House and wanted something wrapped. He looked at me and barked, 'You, wrap that!' and pointed to some object. I just thought, you rude, ignorant sod, and felt like decking him. But I did what I was told to do even though it surprised me to have someone so senior, but less senior than the Queen Mother, saying something in a way that she never would have. She would have asked politely, 'Colin, is there any chance you might find some wrapping paper and wrap that present for me; that would be nice?' At that moment, I rather felt that the yin and yang of life was somehow a bit topsy-turvy.

Andrew was affected. I got the impression that he wanted you to know he was a Royal and therefore important. He seemed quite insecure, but this could be attributed to the simplest of things, such as middle-child syndrome, because being a middle child he got rather lost in those around him. He was unable to relax and gave the impression of never being off-duty. He always seemed to be rushing around and as if he were very preoccupied with one thing or another. I felt he was there for himself and himself only. The only time I ever had anything approaching a cordial chat with him was when he telephoned me at Birkhall to ask about the weather conditions because he wanted to fly up and land his helicopter in the grounds there. But it never went beyond a quick climate report.

I saw Sarah Ferguson rarely and that was when I was at Balmoral. She would be dropping off her daughters, Beatrice and Eugenie, for the weekend. She was always very nice and very pleasant, the complete opposite of Andrew, and would pop inside for half an hour to have a chat with the Queen before leaving. I don't think Andrew, to this day, has ever got over their split. He still loves her very deeply. She is the fun that's missing in his life. So Andrew just carries on, struggling – even now, I think – to find his real identity and role in life. He's not going to inherit the Crown and the combination of that and being a middle child has made him a bit whiney and temperamental. But it is easy to criticise members of the Royal Family, so it's important to remember that despite all his faults he has done a lot of real things that other people would not be able to do, like flying a helicopter through gunfire to pick up soldiers in the Falklands, and while no human being has the right to be arrogant and brutish with anyone, he was just the way he was and he wasn't going to change.

Edward, on the other hand, is completely different from both Charles and Andrew. He is a very sincere man who, I discovered, was a rather reluctant Royal. I got the feeling he would rather be a normal kind of bloke than one who was trapped in the royal goldfish bowl. He never quite got to grips with the etiquette and formality. I remember on the day of Trooping the Colour in 1995, the Royal Family was taken as usual to Horse Guards' Parade to watch the ceremony from a balcony. All the Royal Family were there, enjoying a drink inside, and Sir Ralph Anstruther arrived in a carriage with the Queen Mother. Now, there is a quaint tradition whereby, if one is part of the royal party, one doesn't have to acknowledge the royal salute by taking one's hat off. In this way, one is recognising that it is not you who is being saluted but the person you are with. So Ralph turned up with the Queen Mother and a royal salute was given, which, because it was for the Queen Mother, he didn't acknowledge, but as he walked into the room, he was accosted by Edward who, half-smiling, said, 'Oh, Ralph. Hello, Ralph.' Ralph nodded and Edward added, 'Ah,

Ralph, erm, I spotted that you didn't acknowledge the royal salute on your way in.'

Ralph seemed to bristle at the impertinence of this young fellow questioning his knowledge of etiquette and told him, 'I know, Your Highness. That is because when one is travelling with a royal personage, one doesn't acknowledge the royal salute.'

In his typical jovial fashion, Edward gave him a cheeky dig and said, 'Oh, that sounds a likely story to me, Ralph.' It was only when he noticed Ralph getting more and more red-faced that he told him, 'Well, it sounds like a good enough story. All right, I suppose that's okay then,' and escaped before Ralph blew.

Recovering his composure, Ralph slowly turned to where I was standing and with a smile on his face said in a low tone, 'Cheeky boy.'

But every one of the staff was very fond of Edward, who is quite a sensitive person and a lot more emotional than Charles and Andrew, which is a very non-royal trait. He was a very caring and sharing type of guy, who saw the Queen Mother about as often as Andrew did, but unlike Andrew, he would stop and have a chat and a joke with the staff. He knew what life was all about – after all, this was a guy who was running a television production company in Soho. So he was fairly worldly wise; you had to be, running a production company for five years as he did. He wasn't a total innocent and he had his feet firmly on the ground. When he visited Clarence House, he was a breath of fresh air compared to Andrew. Andrew had his feet firmly on the ground only to the extent that any military officer could have, because if you have spent your life in the forces, you are not really in tune with modern society; rather, you are in tune with a very archaic organisation which mirrors the same sort of old-fashioned values that the Royal Family does.

Edward was not a military type but he was in awe of the military and the royal system in general. He would be quietly respectful towards anyone of high rank and somewhat deferential in their company. This was the opposite of Charles and Andrew who had done their military service and could hold their own in any company. Edward always recognised that he never really made it in the military, or any other working role come to that. He seemed to have a whole host of different careers, flitting one way then another, without actually settling on one thing. To some extent my heart went out to him because there was absolutely nothing he could do about his situation. He was born into royalty and that was that. He didn't enjoy making royal visits and would much rather have carved out a career for himself, but unfortunately when he did pursue a career, people tended to shoot him down for being part of the Royal Family, as if his television career were simply a hobby. He couldn't win, but he managed to cope with it quite well.

Anne was very much like Edward. She was possibly the quietest of the Queen Mother's grandchildren and one whom I hardly saw at all. In the two years that I was equerry, I think she came to Clarence House just once. The few times I did see her she came across as being very astute, with a dry sense of humour. She would throw you little glances as she gave a witty aside, or give you a sly little smile as she uttered some comment. She was completely unaffected by her position as a royal and was a genuine, honest person, there was no doubt about that, and she was a person with very few airs and graces. There have been stories in the past in the press about her lack of fashion sense and this is true to a point, but she didn't really seem to care about fashion or what she looked like. I remember one evening when she was on her way to a party and she had a very flowing, puffy kind of ball gown on, but she had offset this with a bright red G-Shock watch. It was really bright. So instead of your eyes being drawn to her flamboyant dress, all you saw was this rather crazy-looking watch. But she couldn't care less if it didn't go with the dress. If she wanted to wear a bright red watch, she would bloody well wear one. I said to her, 'Are you expecting heavy rain?'

She looked at me as if I had gone bonkers and said, 'What?'

I added, 'You've got your waterproof G-Shock watch on.'

And she just said, 'Oh,' looked at it and laughed, because she hadn't even noticed she was wearing it. That made it even better.

It was a slightly eccentric thing to do. But with things such as the G-Shock watch, she just thought, well, that's the sort of thing I wear, so I'll wear it. I just thought her unaffectedness was brilliant. She didn't have to prove herself to anyone or anything; she just did what she wanted to do. This attitude was reflected in her relationship with the Queen Mother's staff because, like Edward and Charles, she was very chatty with the entire household.

Of all the Queen Mother's grandchildren, my personal favourite was Princess Margaret's son, Viscount Linley. To me, he was one of, if not the most, impressive members of the Royal Family. He ran his own furniture business and had a real skill for spotting business opportunities. If you look at his products, they are all of great quality because he is a skilled craftsman himself. When he visited the Queen Mother, which was almost as often as Charles, you got the impression that here was a man who was very friendly and very worldly wise. He enjoyed life and had a large number of sports cars and motorbikes. He was always very funny and to the point and as far removed from the stereotypical bumbling aristocrat as you could ever get. I got on well with him and he would often have a story or two to tell me about someone he was doing business with, or he would bring in a sample of a product he was working on for me to look at. He blended the modern world he lived in with the old-fashioned royal way of life perfectly and came across as a regular guy.

I could see a bit of David Linley in Prince William. Of the Queen Mother's great-grandchildren, William was the one she saw the most, followed by his younger brother, Harry. They were frequent visitors when we were up in Scotland and William popped into Clarence House once every couple of weeks. I remember spotting this elaborate Limoges duck on a sideboard at Clarence House and saying to Alastair, 'Oh, that's wonderful.'

Alastair said, 'Yes, I know. But we had real problems with that because about four years ago William popped round on a visit and smashed it with a toy hammer. I had to get it mended before the Queen Mother found out.'

Later, at a dinner party, I said to the Queen Mother, 'It's a shame about the duck and what happened to it.'

She looked at me with a quizzical expression and said, 'Why, what happened to it?'

I quickly glanced over at Alastair who was discreetly shaking his head from side to side. It was hardly discernible but I knew exactly what he meant and I suddenly fell silent.

The Queen Mother said, 'I'm not supposed to know, am I?' and started laughing.

'No,' I said, 'feeling deeply embarrassed.

'Well, don't tell then,' she added with a smile.

Apart from going on destruction missions with a toy hammer, William was a very nice chap, who by then was in his early teens. He came to Clarence House with his father, Charles, and was a very polite and enthusiastic young lad. I taught him to juggle, though I can't recall him ever doing it in public, which is a shame because he is quite good. I took my juggling balls all over the place with me; they were a hangover from my Army days to help me with my co-ordination. I taught him at Birkhall where he first saw me juggling and said, 'That's pretty good, can I have a go?'

He was a quick learner and shows the same interest in life and things in general as Prince Charles, and he's going to be very much like his father in later life. When he came to see the Queen Mother, he was always very affectionate with her and she cared about him deeply, especially because of everything that was going on in his life concerning his parents. But, with such a massive generation gap, she did find it difficult to understand half the things William and Harry would say to her. William would talk to her about films, computer games and the usual things that boys of his age would chat about and that most parents wouldn't understand. And she would just look at him and say, 'Nice, oh, that is nice,' when in reality she didn't have a clue what he was going on about.

William had a fantastic relationship with Charles, who tried to be as normal a father as possible under the quite restrictive circumstances they found themselves in. It was lovely to see because there was a real bond between the pair. Every time I saw Charles and William together, they were full of love for each other and would give each other hugs. Perhaps because Prince Charles lived in fear of his father, Prince Philip, when he was a child and couldn't really get close to his mother because she was always busy with affairs of State, he made a conscious effort to ensure that the same thing didn't happen with his children. As a result, William could be a bit mischievous, viz the Limoges duck incident, but deep down he was just doing what every boy his age did. There wasn't much for him to do at Clarence House, so I, being the closest in age, would keep him entertained by chatting with him and telling him jokes. Obviously, at Birkhall there was a bit more to do and William would go off shooting. He was too young to stalk stags, so instead he would pop off rabbits with a .22 rifle, and he really enjoyed it. He seemed to like Balmoral and Birkhall very much because he could do his own thing whether it was shooting rabbits or a bit of fishing, and he was quite mature for his age in this respect.

Harry was just a bit too young at that time. He was still maturing and didn't visit the Queen Mother as much as William, so I didn't really establish a relationship with him. He just seemed to tag along with his brother.

CHAPTER NINE

PRINCESS MARGARET IS ON FIRE

The Queen Mother's children, Elizabeth and Margaret, were rather like her grandchildren in that they had widely different personality traits. The Queen was like her mother. She was a stickler for etiquette and tradition but also had this slightly wicked side. In contrast, Margaret was a bit of a wild card and had a short temper, a bit like Andrew, and when I was there she was entering what I think of as her accident years. The difference between them can perhaps best be summed up during a royal get-together at Sandringham over Christmas. The family was having dinner and during the meal Princess Margaret leaned to get something and her hair moved in the way of a candle. Almost without it being noticed, her hair started smouldering and before long caught the Queen's attention.

It took only about ten seconds for the back of the

Queen's sister's head to start blazing away and Margaret knew nothing about it. The Queen, in slight amusement, turned and said, 'Oh look, Margo's on fire!'

A quick-thinking member of staff patted it out with his hands while Margaret looked at him in horror as if to say, 'What the hell do you think you are doing, do you know who I am?' It was only when it was pointed out to her what had actually happened that her face changed from horror to one of genuine shock and concern for herself. I'm surprised she didn't know by the smell of the burnt hair, which isn't pleasant, I can vouch for that. In a way, it pre-empted the time, a few years later, when she had a nasty accident getting into a scalding bath, which happened just after I had left Clarence House. She ran the bath herself, didn't test it and just got straight in. It was boiling hot and she scalded herself badly.

But the Queen's reaction to her sister catching fire was typical. When people have accidents, when they fall over or trip up, it's sometimes very hard to stop yourself laughing, even if they may have hurt themselves, and the Queen was very much the laughing sort. She saw humour in potential tragedy. She is extremely bright, very much so, and very funny. I was really quite lucky to spend so much time in her presence, but I did so because as an equerry I wasn't just contracted to look after the Queen Mother, I was part of a team responsible for any member of royalty and this included the Head of State. And the Queen, if I ever turned up at one of her dinner parties, would always make a bee-line for me and say: 'Colin, how are you? It's great to see you.'

The Queen was very friendly and she is so knowledgeable about everything from art to history to politics; you name it, she knows something about it. Her knowledge of current affairs is second to none, unlike the Queen Mother's, and the Queen would let her opinions be known. She is quite forthright. Obviously, in public she is guarded, but in private she does speak her mind, and she doesn't approve of the current trend of making press statements which she feels that, on occasion, she has been bounced into doing. The best example of this was during the aftermath of the death of Princess Diana when there was a massive public clamouring for her to address the nation, which she did in the end, but rather reluctantly. But she is not a timid person by any stretch of the imagination. She just recognises that there is a time and a place for everything.

One of the most memorable encounters I had with her was during pre-dinner drinks at Balmoral, when she started telling me about the time Michael Fagan broke into her bedroom back in July 1982. I remember saying to her, 'That must have been very scary for you.'

'Oh no,' she said with a smile, 'I wasn't scared in the slightest.'

She added, 'When I woke, I just saw him there at the end of my bed and for a split second I thought it was a member of staff. A second later, I realised it was somebody from the outside.'

She said, 'As soon as I realised this, I thought, oh well, I'll just have to talk to him.'

What did slightly alarm her was when she realised he was dripping blood from a nasty gash on his hand. She told me:

'I just asked him what he was doing in my bedroom. He said he had come to chat and so we chatted. I asked him his name and about his life and his family. To be honest I didn't really have much time to be alarmed.'

Eventually she said she told him, 'Look, you really shouldn't be here.'

He replied, 'Yes, I know.'

There then followed a farcical situation in which she picked up the phone and asked the operator manning the palace switchboard to contact the police. The message was passed on but the police didn't respond. So the Queen continued chatting to him and she said to me, 'He asked me about my children and I said I had four and gave their names. Then we chatted about his children.'

She then tried to summon a chambermaid by pressing a button. Again, no one came.

'He asked for a cigarette,' she told me, 'but I said I didn't smoke.'

Eventually a chambermaid did enter the Queen's chamber only to see Fagan, rush out in horror and get a footman who seized him. All the time, as the Queen told me, they 'just carried on talking'.

She added, 'Really, Colin, I wasn't scared. The whole thing was so surreal. He just came in, we chatted and then he went without incident, and that was that.'

But I think it did rattle her because when he had gone she got up and had a couple of whiskies and asked an awful lot of questions of her security. At that time, it was becoming a major problem – twelve months earlier a man had fired six blanks at her during the Trooping the Colour ceremony, and now Fagan had managed to breach security for a second time, the first being a month before when he had stolen a bottle of wine from the palace.

So she had every reason to question security. Fagan had managed to climb a fourteen-foot high wall that was topped with barbed wire and spikes at 6.00 in the morning. He was spotted by an off-duty policeman but, by the time the policeman had told the palace guards, Fagan couldn't be found. He got into the palace through an open window and found himself in King George V's stamp collection room, which contains stamps valued at £14 million, but the door out of the room was locked so he went back out through the window, setting off alarms as he entered and exited the room, which a policeman inside the palace picked up on but put down to a malfunction and turned off, twice! The farce continued when, back outside, Fagan climbed a drainpipe, pulled back some wire meant to keep pigeons away and climbed into the office of Vice Admiral Sir Peter Ashmore, who was the man responsible for the Queen's safety. He then walked down a hallway admiring the priceless paintings on show and pausing to say good morning to a housekeeper before entering the Queen's bedroom. Under normal circumstances, an armed guard stands outside the Queen's door at night and when his shift finishes at 6.00 in the morning he is replaced by an unarmed footman. The footman was out walking the Queen's corgis – could you imagine the look on his face when he got back, my God! – and there was some suggestion that Fagan wanted to harm the Queen because along the way he had picked up an ashtray and smashed it in half, so he was effectively armed as he walked in. But, as the Queen told me, she simply kept him talking until help arrived.

Underlying her façade is a woman who simply isn't the shy and retiring type. This is someone who shoots and fishes and is very socially adept. So, when confronted with a potential killer, she put her social skills to good use and kept him talking. There was also some suggestion that Fagan was going to commit suicide in her bedroom but decided it wasn't 'a nice thing to do' once he got chatting to her.

Fagan seemed to see in her what I saw in the Queen Mother, and it was interesting to watch the Queen interacting with her mother. They had a wonderful relationship that was built on deep affection and respect for each other. There's a wonderful story of them lunching together when the Queen asked for another glass of wine only for her mother to frown and say, 'Is that wise? You know you have to reign all afternoon.'

Neither of them curtsied to the other, and if the Queen Mother said anything that her daughter found amusing, the Queen would say 'Oh Mummy', and laugh.

They would sometimes be in hoots over something or other. When they were together, they often fed the dogs biscuits shaped like little Hovis loaves. If guests were present they would be given a couple of biscuits, too, not to eat themselves, but to give to the dogs. But so many guests fell foul of this. The Queen or the Queen Mother would give a few biscuits to the guests who would then sit with them on their plate after lunch or dinner, and you could see them looking round at the other guests wondering what the biscuits were for before gingerly picking them up to eat. Suddenly the Queen or Queen Mother would shout, 'No, no, no, they're for the dogs.'

Nearly every guest made this mistake. They thought it was an extra course, albeit a very strange one. The Queen and Queen Mother could easily have avoided this by telling them what the biscuits were for as they handed them out, but their naughty streak often got the better of them.

When I was with the Queen, I sometimes found myself doing a double take and asking myself, am I really here? When you met the Queen Mother you went into 'Queen Mother mode', but with the Queen it was different. With the Queen Mother you weren't so familiar with her because you hadn't seen as many pictures and photographs of her in newspapers and on television as you had with the Queen. The Queen is such a familiar face, you rather feel you know her the moment you are introduced and within minutes you feel used to her and totally at ease in her presence. I suspect the same comparison could be applied to someone like Tom Cruise or another top Hollywood star. You feel you know everything about them, including the lines on their face because you have seen them so often on television and at the cinema. But because you were not so used to the Queen Mother or her facial features, you would find yourself gazing at her and thinking, God, this is the Queen Mother. I know I did. I would sometimes have to stop myself because I realised that I had been studying her when I should have been chatting to guests.

The Queen, like the Queen Mother, was very good at making you feel comfortable. She did this in a number of ways. More often than not it involved commenting on the tie or a pair of cufflinks that a particular guest was wearing. She was really lovely to talk to. The Queen Mother was very good at throwing knowing looks if someone said something that she disagreed with or found controversial or which she just didn't understand. It was all nods and winks with the Queen Mother. You didn't get that at all with the Queen. She was a lot more worldly and knew what a pedestrian crossing was for a start. The Queen had been brought up to know how things worked.

I saw the Queen mainly at Sandringham and Balmoral. She never really came to Clarence House, although she did talk to her mother by phone on a daily basis. At Balmoral, she loved the picnic lunches and it was nice to see her relaxed. I have read that she is quite conservative in her ways and, for example, would live off just porridge if she could. This is absolute rubbish. She loved her food, though she was quite keen on porridge, I must say. But all the Royal Family tend to go for the same sort of thing. They all loved their crayfish, the egg starters and nursery puddings such as chocolate mousse. It's obviously something they have been brought up on. The Queen also liked a gin and tonic, though she is not a heavy drinker.

One of the Queen's biggest highlights of the year was the build-up to Christmas. At Sandringham, they had a huge table and every year a massive jigsaw puzzle was put out with the box on the side as a guide. Anyone who walked past would be invited to do a piece of the jigsaw. It was a huge thing, about 10,000 pieces, and the Queen would spend hours doing it. She loved puzzles; that was her big thing, especially at Christmas. About forty per cent of the Christmas jigsaw would be done by guests, the other sixty per cent was the work of the Queen. She would also spend a lot of time reading the papers. She had to, really, in order to discuss affairs of State once a week with the prime minister. Her paper of choice was the *Daily Telegraph*, but she also made sure she read all the tabloids. They were a useful tool for her in gauging the mood of the nation. Her other main interest was television. She did enjoy *EastEnders* and soaps in general and, like the Queen Mother, she enjoyed having her dinner on a tray in front of the television.

But her relationship with her children was different, especially with Charles. It was very formal. It was nothing like the close relationship he had with the Queen Mother, which was a much cosier affair. The Queen's position means that anyone, including other members of the Royal Family such as Prince Charles, should bow in respect. The Queen is also surrounded by a lot of formality and Charles, even though he is her son, has to respect this. But he just called the Queen Mother 'Granny' and tradition went out of the window. No matter how much he wanted to, it seemed sometimes that Charles just couldn't get close to the Queen. That is why, whenever he saw me, all he talked about was the Queen Mother. He found her awesome. I never once heard him talking about his mother.

I felt slightly sorry for Prince Charles in this respect because on the one hand he had his mother to whom he couldn't get near and on the other there was his father, Prince Philip, a giant of a man who was very forthright in his opinions and not afraid to speak his mind. I was wary of him so God only knows what Charles thought. I remember being at a party with Prince Andrew's equerry when Philip came up to him. He had spotted the tie he was wearing and said, 'Ah, you were in the Navy, where were you stationed then?'

Andrew's equerry said, 'Oh, I'm sorry, this does look like a Navy tie but it's not, it's my old school tie. A lot of people have mistaken it for…'

But before he had chance to finish his sentence Prince Philip said, 'Ah,' and had walked off.

He was one of these people who had absolutely no time for chit-chat. I would go so far as to say that he didn't like chattering to people at all. He just went straight to the point and couldn't see any reason for beating about the bush. He didn't suffer fools and no one, and I mean no one, not even the Queen, could force him to say the right thing or do anything he didn't want to do.

A story told to me at Clarence House by one of the junior members of staff sums him up well. It was when Prince Andrew was a young boy of eight. Every time he came out of Buckingham Palace, the guards would have to salute him. Well, Andrew picked up on this and kept running outside taking great pleasure in having this one particular guard salute him relentlessly while he blew raspberries in his face. In the end, the guard said to him, 'Look, get lost.'

So Andrew did get lost, only to come back with his father, who said to the guard, 'I understand you told my son to get lost?'

To which the guard replied: 'I did, Your Highness.'

'Well, why did you tell him to get lost. Come on, tell me,' Prince Philip blasted.

And the guard, fearing his palace career was now over and he had nothing to lose, said, 'Well, he kept blowing raspberries at me and every time he comes out I have to salute him and he's come out about twenty times now in the space of a couple of minutes.'

Prince Philip, whose face had been getting red listening to this explanation, turned to Andrew and shouted, 'Well, you've heard the man. Go on, get lost.'

I very rarely saw the Queen and Prince Philip together when I was at Clarence House, perhaps just a couple of times during my two years in the job. When he came up to Birkhall for the summer, Prince Philip was often alone and he would potter off by himself doing work on the estate. He would occasionally go shooting and fishing, but most of his time was spent running the estate. He acted as a very hands-on estate manager and ran everything. The Queen didn't want to get too involved in what I would term the mucky side of things, but Philip did. He loved doing physical work and getting stuck in.

I wouldn't say he was un-PC, although I do appreciate he has said things in the past that haven't been politically correct. But he was never like that with me. He was actually quite engaging, though he was a stickler for formality and really knew the ropes.

If anything, the Queen seemed to be closer to her dogs than she was to Philip. She certainly spent more time with them and had fourteen corgis – which are Welsh cattle dogs – and the Queen Mother had four. One of the highlights of their day in Scotland was feeding the dogs sausages. Every single day, just before lunch and dinner, the dogs would gather round their feet and the sausages would come out. And throughout the day they were fed tidbits so they got quite fat, and snappy with it, too, snappier than a crocodile handbag. You could stroke them, but if they were in a bad mood you learned to avoid them. I saw them really go for some people. They would bite their ankles and things like that. The Queen Mother's corgis would growl at people they didn't like, and they took a dislike to lots of visitors. But the Queen Mother would immediately put a stop to this by saying something like, 'Oh, Ranger, must you?' which would shut them up almost straight away.

Historically it was the Queen Mother's husband, King George VI, who first had corgis. He got them during the War, together with some Labradors. The Queen grew up with them and simply fell in love with the breed, which explains why she has so many. But it was only the Queen and Queen Mother who had them. The Prince of Wales likes Jack Russells. When he becomes king, I imagine he'll have the corgis mashed into royal dog food; I doubt very much you will see corgis at the palace again when Charles succeeds to the throne. Jack Russells will then become the royal dog of choice. The only other Royal who was keen on dogs was Princess Anne. She kept English bull-terriers, which were a source of even more controversy than the snappy corgis. In 2004, Anne's four-year-old bull-terrier Dotty went for the Queen's corgi Pharos at Sandringham. Dotty already had form. She had attacked two boys at Windsor Great Park the year before for which the Princess Royal was fined £500 and had to pay a similar amount in compensation. The dog became too much to handle in the end and had to be put down.

The corgis were rather like the Queen in the way they seemed to carry with them this touch of formality, if dogs can have such a thing. This was echoed in the Queen's demeanour. She was the Queen and she was never really off duty. Instead, she had to adhere to a clearly defined role that carried with it certain standards of behaviour and attitude. Margaret, on the other hand, was more feisty and opinionated and generally a bit noisier than her older sister. She was certainly more personable and also flirtatious. She did like to enjoy herself and would often poke fun at people and be a little bit more down-to-earth than her sister. There was more of a chumminess and chattiness about her. But, on the other hand, if you said something that she disagreed with, she would reply, 'Oh that is absolute nonsense,' and almost cut you off in mid sentence.

She could get quite snappy and her mood could turn on a sixpence. One minute she would be all smiles and the next she would be crotchety and snappy. People were very aware of this and trod carefully around her. She could even be crotchety with both the Queen and Queen Mother and it didn't take much for them to expose her short temper. She even had a go at me once or twice for not doing something fast enough. She would say, 'Come on, come on, you're too slow. Speed up a bit.' I just let it go over my head. I did whatever she wanted me to do with gritted teeth and then just walked away. The Queen Mother was more subtle. Instead of being short with you, she would just give you a look or even smile at you. But it wasn't a smile of satisfaction, it was more of a grimace. It took me a few months to work out what this actually meant – that even though she was smiling she wasn't really very happy with something you had done. When she did this to me, I thought, oh my God, here we go. And I would just crumble.

You would never get that from the Queen. You never really saw chinks in her armour. But Margaret, like Edward, Anne and the other minor Royals had a bit more leverage in their emotions. Even so, I think they all found it slightly frustrating to have none of the benefits afforded the senior Royals and yet a lot of the headaches. And it did annoy them, especially Edward, not to be able to do their own thing all the time and to have their lives constantly scrutinised by the media. Margaret found herself very much part of this bubble, but often eschewed protocol to get her own way. I remember her saying to me one morning: 'Ah, Colin, what are you doing this morning?'

'Well, nothing really,' I replied.

'Great, well, grab your swimming trunks. Come on, let's

go for a swim and then we'll come back and have lunch.'

I was a bit taken aback by this and blurted out, 'Crikey, okay then!'

All the time I wondered what protocol dictated about how you were supposed to swim with a female member of the Royal Family. But this was Margaret, a woman who led quite a hedonistic lifestyle and came across as someone who had lived a bit, so I thought, what the hell, I'll go with the flow. At that stage, there was no real sign of the health problems that were to plague her in later years. Although she did smoke a bit, she was still quite active for her age. So we loaded up a Range Rover and went to one of her friends' houses that had an outdoor pool. I was in the pool, when she appeared in this rather old-fashioned, one-piece swimming outfit and I spent the rest of the morning feeling very uncomfortable. I tried to swim in such a way that I was always on the opposite side of the pool to her. I just didn't want to get too close.

It was a very strange situation to be in after spending a year in a quite reserved and quite stuffy environment to be then literally thrown into a swimming pool with Princess Margaret. It wasn't very enjoyable because it seemed a tad too informal and a bit too close for my comfort.

The interaction between Princess Margaret and the Queen was quite fascinating. They were very natural with each other and very, very relaxed in each other's company; they acted as all sisters did. They were there for each other, they confided in each other and whenever they were together, I found myself almost switching off. It was as though I wasn't working for the Royal Family anymore but just an ordinary family, albeit with all the trappings of wealth. They chatted away and would be very much in family mode, but there was a reverence and mutual respect between Margaret and the Queen. Margaret did recognise that Elizabeth was the senior of the two and she would curtsey and so on, but this was to show respect for the Crown rather than curtseying because it was her sister.

CHAPTER TEN

SETTING THE
HOUNDS ON THE BOYS
FROM ETON

'On the word go, I want you all to start running,' said the new Eton College headmaster, John Lewis.

The boys, about a dozen in all, were dressed in their PE kit.

'Go,' he said.

And they were off, running full pelt across the lawns of Royal Lodge in Windsor Great Park with a pack of hounds in full pursuit.

The Queen Mother loved it. Her eyes lit up. I found it all a bit odd; it was all a bit 'Tomkinson's Schooldays' from Michael Palin's TV comedy *Ripping Yarns*. One boy was struggling at the back and soon the hounds were upon him, jumping at him and barking. But instead of tearing him to pieces as they would a fox, they virtually licked him to death. All the boys got the same treatment. It was part of a tradition that the Queen Mother put on to welcome any new Eton headmaster, though what the boys thought of it is anyone's guess.

Most of the Queen Mother's weekends were spent at Royal Lodge and she loved getting out of London. She didn't like the capital at all. I was present very occasionally because normally I was allowed weekends off. But I was drafted in for the odd party or lunch, of which the headmaster's visit was one. Royal Lodge, situated within the grounds of the park, was a nice escape for her and she would tell me, 'I just love the peace and tranquillity of the place.'

The Lodge itself is situated half a mile south east of Windsor Castle and the Queen Mother had been using it since 1952. The site itself dates back to 1662, when a house was built there and then gradually improved and rebuilt over time. In 1931, it was granted to the Queen Mother and her husband, as the Duke and Duchess of York, and after the King's death, she continued to use it as her weekend retreat. The main building is quite imposing with some thirty rooms, including seven bedrooms and a saloon, and the grounds extend over more than 90 acres.

Royal Lodge allowed the Queen Mother some quiet time and she was well served by her third senior butler, an ex-RAF steward who went by the name of Wellbeloved. The funny thing was that unlike with William and Reg, I never got to know his first name. Wellbeloved looked after Royal Lodge and was on the same level as the two other senior butlers, even though I got the impression that William and Reg never really rated him. I found him brilliant and so much easier to deal with; because he was the only one at the

Lodge, getting things arranged was often much simpler. And you didn't have to worry about his emotions so much because, like me, he was ex-military and preferred to be more straightforward about taking instructions.

I enjoyed my occasional visits to Royal Lodge much more than being at Clarence House. It was at the Lodge that I taught one of the Queen Mother's sixty-five-year-old friends how to rollerblade. We were chatting with the Queen Mother about ballet and she just brought it up completely out of the blue and told her friend, 'Did you know Colin rollerblades? I imagine you need similar poise and skill to do that.'

Her friend said, 'Oh, I would love to do that.'

So I said, 'Well, I can arrange it.'

And I got one of the chauffeurs to drive back to London and pick up my rollerblades and buy a second pair on the return journey. Then later that day, I took her out in the grounds of Royal Lodge and taught her how to rollerblade. The Queen Mother watched us and every few minutes she offered words of encouragement, saying, 'Oh, that's fantastic' and 'Isn't that brilliant'.

She loved moments like that. It reminded me of when she was asked what was the secret of her longevity, and she famously said, 'I love life. That's the secret. It is the exhilaration of others that keeps me going. Sometimes I feel drained, you do at my age, but excitement is good for me.'

She was most alive during her annual holiday at Birkhall, which is part of the Balmoral estate in the Scottish Highlands. Birkhall is gorgeous. By royal standards, it is quite a modest house which is sheltered by the wooded hills of Royal Deeside and stands on the fringes of the estate overlooking the salmon-rich River Muick. The Queen Mother described it as 'a small big house, or a big small house', and it was done up very much in her taste with tartan on the walls and floors, *Spy* cartoons in the passages and outdoor clothes flung on chapel hat pegs. Every hour, the tranquillity of the place would be shattered by eleven grandfather clocks all chiming, though not quite in unison, in the dining room.

The house itself was built in 1715 and the Royal Family bought it from the Abergeldie family in 1849. In 1930, King George V lent it to the Queen Mother and her husband, who redecorated it and landscaped the gardens. It has remained a favourite bolthole of the Royals ever since. Princess Alexandra and Sir Angus Ogilvy honeymooned there in 1968, as did Princess Margaret's daughter Lady Sarah Chatto, some years later. Prince Charles took Princess Diana up there in the weeks before he proposed to her, and later Charles and Camilla Parker Bowles used it to stage manage the first 'proper' meeting between Princes William and Harry and Tom and Laura Parker Bowles.

But holiday may not be the best way of describing the time I spent up there, certainly not for me because I found it stamina sapping. We would go up to Birkhall at the end of July and I would take three weeks off in September before returning to Scotland until the beginning of November when we would all go back to Clarence House. In Scotland, my day would start at 7.00 in the morning when I would come down for breakfast and make sure that everything was in place for the guests and the Queen Mother, or any other member of the Royal Family who was present. Once breakfast was underway, I would go off and sort out the Land Rovers for the guests and allocate them a ghillie – the person charged with looking after them for the day. They would be given rods if they wanted to go fishing and the ghillie would sort them out with tackle, or guns if they wanted to shoot. The ghillie was there to cater for their every need. Then I would tell everyone which cottage we would be meeting up at for lunch. There were about seven of them dotted around the estate and the Queen Mother liked to take it in turns eating in them. Lunch would generally be around 1.00 in the afternoon, and the guests would all toddle off around 9.30 to do their thing, whether it was hunting, shooting or fishing, while some would just go walking. I would be left to do some paperwork in the house where I had my own office, before going fishing for an hour or two on the Muick.

I must admit I was new to fishing when I first came to Birkhall and had never fly-fished before. It's a much bigger deal than fishing with a float. I would be wearing waders, standing in water that was waist deep and thinking, if I slip on a rock, I don't think I'll be able to get up and I might possibly drown. It was bloody hard work. You could fish all day and not get anything. If you caught one, it was put in a bag by one of the ghillies and everyone ate it later. The chefs would turn it into a kedgeree or something. But I have to say that standing in a cold river for a few hours waiting for my feet to go numb while I desperately failed to catch a fish didn't really thrill me. Unfortunately, I was required to do some fishing; it was expected of me. The Queen Mother would say; 'Oh, Colin, you must go fishing.' She loved it. So what was I going to do, turn round and say no?

Afterwards, I would meet up with the Queen Mother at one of the cottages for lunch. Her favourite was a lodge right next to the Muick and, after lunch, guests would go fishing on it and she would watch them. The lodges were not particularly well kitted out and were shut up for most of the year. Once summer came, I would go up and unlock them and give them a good airing. Before lunch, when I met her at one of these places, the Queen Mother was generally alone. She usually turned up wearing her favourite hat, which was a blue one with a small feather in it, although she did wear a stetson for a day that I had brought back with me from America and given to her as a present. Then the two of us would unpack the picnic and lay the table together. She loved putting things out; there were no airs and graces about her. We unpacked bottles of whisky, brandy, gin – you name it, she had it – because we had to be prepared for every request for a drink. So there was a lot of booze. Then we would crack open a bottle of wine, have a sausage and just sit there talking and waiting for the guests to arrive, maybe for half an hour, sometimes for an hour.

One of my favourite guests was Ted Hughes, who was the then Poet Laureate. He had such an amazing mind and was very, very intelligent. I remember telling him that one of the first books I ever read was *The Iron Man*. The next day he pulled me to one side and said, 'There you go, Colin,' and gave me a signed copy of the book with a message inside. He came up to Scotland quite a few times for these lunches. In the evenings, he would read his latest poems. During some of the longer ones, especially once a few glasses of port had been consumed, I would give a sharp cough just towards the end in case anyone had nodded off. By the time Ted looked up from the page, sure enough everyone was smiling and, above all, awake.

If the weather was nice, we sat outside for lunch; if it was raining, we would go into the lodge and a fire was lit. But there was nothing ostentatious about it. Lunches were eaten on trestle tables and it was all very rugged. The lunches would go on until about 3.00 in the afternoon and when they finished I would get the blasted waders on again and go back in the river, this time a little worse for wear after three of four glasses of wine, and do my best to stand up on very slippery rocks that seemed more treacherous after lunch than before it. I did this for a couple of hours, or until exhaustion set in, before going back to Birkhall at about 5.00 pm. If I had enough time, I might go for a game of squash with one of the bodyguards, go for a walk, write some letters, or make a few telephone calls. At 6.00 pm, I would have a shower and forty-five minutes later be in my black tie ready for pre-dinner drinks at 7.00 and to welcome the guests who were staying, arriving, or both. Then the whole dinner routine kicked in again and after dinner the ladies went off to talk, leaving the men to smoke cigars.

After about an hour, everyone joined up again to watch

an episode of *Fawlty Towers* or *Keeping Up Appearances*. This was when the Queen Mother would steal a little nap, unless it was the German episode from *Fawlty Towers*. And while we were all watching television, the butler would go round the place with a pot of burning incense. That was part of his job; it was used to disguise the smell of the cooking. When the Queen Mother retired to bed at between 11.00 pm and midnight, sometimes later, this was the signal for the guests who weren't staying at Birkhall to leave. They would be guided immediately from the living room straight to the front door and I would say, 'Good to see you, have a safe trip back,' and off they would go.

The guests who were staying for two or three nights would almost always want to stay up for a couple more hours and I, as the Queen Mother's representative once she had departed, would be expected to stay up with them until they went to bed. This could be 2.00, 3.00, 4.00 and, on occasions, 5.00 in the morning. And there was guest after guest after guest who stayed that just didn't want to go to bed. It could be the head of Marks and Spencer or WH Smith, whoever. I remember one fellow who brought a Saddam Hussein mask as a laugh. The Queen Mother thought it was hilarious when he put it on and they sat on a sofa and had a ten-minute conversation while he wore it. It was one of the most bizarre sights.

All the guests liked to stay up, drink a bit, chat a lot and sometimes play the piano. And every time I had to be the last man standing when they trotted off to their bedrooms, but no matter what time it was I was never allowed a lie-in and had to be up at 7.00 in the morning. So almost three months of doing this without a day off was pretty tiring and most of the time I felt very weary. It was quite an endurance test. Imagine having a dinner party at home; it takes some preparation. At Birkhall, there were dinner parties every single night. The Queen Mother coped with this like a real trouper. Most ninety-four-year-olds spend their day asleep, but the Queen Mother didn't. She spent her days reading the paper, writing or telephoning friends, going out to picnics, chatting to people and meeting new people and generally led a pretty relentless life. Her routine would cripple most thirty-year-olds. It was non-stop.

Birkhall had its good and bad points that tended to merge into each other. It was good because we were all going to Scotland and living a life that centred on the great outdoors and it wasn't as stuffy as London in terms of formal lunches and the like, plus there wasn't as much office politics going on. Even though there was a permanent staff up there, as at Clarence House, I didn't really have to tread as carefully with them as I did with William and Reg. But even so, the bad point was it was knackering, really knackering.

I quite enjoyed the shooting parts of the trip, but not really grouse shooting. I'm not a great game fan to be honest. Chewing pellets and cracking your teeth on shot doesn't really do a lot for me. Luckily, there were very few grouse up there anyway.

What I did enjoy was stalking, and I came back with quite a few pairs of antlers. Stalking is a really efficient and pretty humane way of culling deer that will otherwise fight each other to the death over limited food. I did a lot of stalking; it was great fun and I killed quite a few deer, but it was quite a bloody process once you had shot one because they were gutted on the spot. Basically, my ghillie would pull the whole of their insides out before strapping the corpse to the back of a couple of ponies to be dragged down the hill to Birkhall. Every part of the deer was used. The meat was eaten by the guests, the hooves were sold to China, the eye balls were sold to Saudi Arabia and even the skins were used in various ways. There wasn't a piece of the animal left by the time they had finished with it. It was very much after the heart of Hugh Fearnley-Whittingstall and it was great.

Some people may be horrified reading this, and even when I was there I made myself a bit unpopular with some of the Royals because I'm not very pro-hunting, unlike the Queen Mother who has shot big game in Africa. Personally, I can see much more efficient ways of killing them – there was recently an article in the *Evening Standard* about a man who now hires himself out with his silenced sniper rifle and kills foxes from your garden for £250. Surely that is the best way of killing them rather than chasing them across fields with packs of dogs. The pro-hunting lobby say that hunting is the most efficient method; well, come on, of course it's not. However, I do understand that fox hunting is a tradition and livelihoods are built around it, and also that foxes cause farmers great trouble. So why not shoot them or gas them instead? I'm sure there are lots of other ways of doing it rather than having fifty or so people spend all day running around the countryside just to catch one fox. There was no fox hunting up in Scotland, although there was in Windsor. I had the opportunity to go on a hunt but turned it down.

I can relate more to why stags have to be shot because they need to be culled for the good of their herd. If you see two stags fighting on the side of a hill because there are too many of them and not enough food, it really is awful to watch. They fight with their antlers and end up poking eyes out and ripping each other apart until one of them dies. The other one is more often than not so badly wounded that it dies later, and, much as I think it's a shame to have to cull any animal, I guess if you are going to do it, shooting them in the head with a rifle is as good a way as any. Stag hunting brought out the Army man in me. I would stick on a combat outfit and spend most of the day trying to get close to a stag that can smell you and see you but which you can't see. Ultimately, when you do see it, it won't be in a position where you can shoot it and it will more than likely run away. I loved the thrill of spotting an elderly stag, the ones you try to cull first, and stalking it sometimes for a full day. I ended up crawling through mud, brambles and streams and at the end was completely exhausted. Most times, they do get away, but when you do manage to shoot a stag all you are doing is making it easier for the rest of the pack to get food. As a soldier, I enjoyed it. When I was up on a hill and the chase was on, it was a challenge.

I also hunted grouse with hawks which flew over the dogs, though this wasn't half as much fun. The dogs would sniff out the grouse and try to make them fly up and the hawks would hover 100 feet or so above your head waiting to pounce on them. Of course, the grouse weren't stupid and could see the hawks above them. They didn't want to fly because they knew that as soon as they did, the hawk would see them and kill them. But they couldn't stay on the ground because the dogs were coming. So they would kind of hop and fly small distances hoping the hawks didn't see them. When a hawk did spot one, you would hear the sound of rushing wind as it swooped down after its prey. It was one of the most amazing things I have ever seen.

The Queen Mother would visit the hawks and hold them; she loved them. But I don't think any member of the Royal Family stalked at that time. They were all a bit conscious of the animal rights lobby and what people might say. After everything they were going through at that time, they wanted very much to cultivate the right public image. If they were spotted killing animals or birds, the media would have torn them to pieces rather like hounds did a fox. But the Queen Mother was very pro-hunting, even of foxes. She liked the whole hunting, shooting and fishing scene generally, as did the Queen who shot occasionally, though she didn't when I was there. Instead, I often saw her and the Queen Mother together taking their dogs for a walk around Balmoral. When the Queen was in Scotland, she would always walk the dogs, whereas in London it was left to one of her footmen to perform this task. The corgis never went on long walks; they never did anything too energetic. I would always find Minnie, the youngest corgi, lying on my bed at Birkhall. She was lovely, and my favourite.

At Balmoral, the Queen was very much in 'tweedy

mode'. She would potter around the place in a tweed jumper or walking gear. I remember bumping into her once outside and simply not recognising her. She had a scarf wrapped round her head and her hood up and as I passed her I said, 'Good morning.'

She replied, 'Oh, good morning.'

I suddenly thought, I know that voice, and then did a double take and stuttered, 'Oh, sorry, ma'am,' before bowing my head.

I even managed to cock that up. The first time you address the Queen you should refer to her as 'Your Majesty', and as 'ma'am' afterwards. But she had this big smile on her face and found it very funny that I hadn't recognised her.

In Scotland, the Queen was a little more relaxed and informal than at Buckingham Palace and would generally go for a walk each morning. Her days were spent very much like the Queen Mother's. She would entertain and have a lot of picnic lunches, and although I never saw her fish or go stalking, she did shoot grouse.

Of all the Royal Family, apart from the Queen Mother, it was Prince Charles who liked to come up to Birkhall most. He has done a lot of hunting in his life, but when I was there he never went stalking or anything like that. He preferred to draw animals and plants. And he is a very good artist, too. He would go off with his ghillie at the start of the day to a hill and sketch, and that would be it; walking and sketching. I just don't think hunting, fishing and shooting is his bag any more. He tends to go for more sedentary pursuits these days. Scotland is a great retreat for him and I think if he could have, he would have come up for the whole summer. It was definitely his favourite place. This was where he escaped the miseries of his life, which had started at Gordonstoun and continued through his first marriage. He hates London but loves Scotland with a passion and he truly enjoys the chance to go out painting and sketching. Its combination of beauty and bleakness seems to suit his character. I saw a definite change in him when he was in Scotland. He was thoroughly at home in the country and wore walking boots, plus-fours and open-neck shirts. Every morning, he would collect his dogs and off he would go into the wilderness. It was a great escape from the nightmares he was having in London. The only time I saw those problems haunt him was that morning at breakfast and the incident with the *Daily Mirror*. That sort of thing dragged him back to reality and depressed him and his response was always the same: 'Oh, bloody hell, why won't they just leave me alone?'

It annoyed him intensely that he was being hounded for no particular reason. But most of the time he was very relaxed and chatty. I managed to have some interesting talks with him about art, people in general and the Army – things he was generally interested in. He was quite a strong character. Any lesser man would have been broken by some of the things that were being said about him.

Similarly, Viscount Linley was a regular visitor to Birkhall and popped up once or twice for a couple of weekends every summer. He, like Charles, was not a 'hunting, shooting or fishing' type and never had been. He would go onto a loch on a speed boat or do something else equally extreme.

Motorboats and speed in general were very much his thing.

I saw Prince Andrew only once up in Scotland and he didn't go hunting either. He just raced around, always on a mission, very much in the same sort of military fashion as he had in London. He was brusque, to the point, focused, energetic, anxious and generally a bit agitated. Edward, like his sister, Anne, never came up and, thinking about it, he would probably have been happier being a pantomime stag rather than having to hunt one.

In between our sojourns at Birkhall, there was a three-week break at the Castle of Mey in Caithness. This was the only home that the Queen Mother owned outright and she obviously liked being there for that very reason. She first saw it in 1952 while mourning the death of the King. When told this ruined, near-derelict, building was to be abandoned she exclaimed, 'Never! It's part of Scotland's heritage. I'll save it.'

When she bought it, the house was surrounded by only 30 acres of parkland which was also in a poor state, and between 1953 and 1955 she set about restoring it. She bought nearby Longoe Farm in 1958 to add to another called Seaview, which she bought in 1956 and which is situated half a mile away and used as overflow accommodation for the castle.

She went to the Castle of Mey for the last couple of weeks in August and for ten days in October. But it was so different from Birkhall. It was remote and situated right on the rugged, windswept and bloody freezing north coast of Scotland. If you sat in the castle, which was more like a big house, and threw your glass out of the window, it would land in the sea. The interior was the only thing that was similar. In décor and general style, neither home was too over the top, just very practical and filled with antique furniture and decorations that had been passed down over generations. Even though we went there in summer, it was always cold and raining. I always rued the fact that it wasn't situated on the Kent coast, which could have made it a very pleasant place to stay indeed. But the Queen Mother counted Scotland as her native home and when she arrived would say, 'We're back on the old terra cotta,' a joke she had picked up from *Only Fools and Horses*.

She felt completely at one with the whole place. But as far as sports and things to do went it was pretty poor. There were no grouse around the castle, and when I went stalking, it wasn't managed land so I found myself walking through heather that was shoulder deep, and I was dressed in itchy tweed, wearing boots that rubbed and carrying a loaded gun. I really didn't look forward to going up there. It was quite hard work. There wasn't much to shoot and I would spend most days walking endlessly up the hills with three other members of the royal staff or other guests for company, looking for things to blast, and we wouldn't find anything, not a dicky-bird. The picnic lunch with the Queen Mother was the highlight of the day. There were no country clubs nearby, as at Balmoral, where I could play squash or have a sauna, and the nearest town, Wick, was about 20 miles away. So this relentless routine of entertaining people until the early hours continued. My job was to find them something to do in this barren and inhospitable part of the country, and what could you do? If a guest decided he didn't want to go hunting or fishing, I had to arrange something else for him or her to do. A trip to the Orkney Islands was one of my favourite ploys. But my job could hardly be called arduous. I always looked forward to going back to Birkhall because there was so much more variety. Even the dogs seemed bored at the Castle of Mey. They would sit waiting for the Queen Mother outside her office door on some stone steps, sometimes for hours. Very occasionally, we didn't have guests and would have to find ways of entertaining ourselves. One game we played was places we had stayed in. For example, the lady-in-waiting would say, 'Have you ever stayed in a hotel?' Everyone would say yes and the game would continue.

Eventually, you could count on the Queen Mother saying something like, 'Has anyone ever been to the White House? I have.'

Of course, nobody else had, so we would all say no and she would win.

Then the lady-in-waiting said, 'What about an embassy?'

I said no, the Queen Mother said, 'Of course, lots of them.'

Then the Queen Mother added, 'Has anyone stayed in a brothel?'

Everyone looked at each other in stunned silence before laughing and saying no.

Another game we played was charades, which I had been told was a favourite of hers. We did have the occasional game with guests and Prince Charles joined in once or twice. He was quite good. I think he would have made a good actor because he could improvise very well. The Queen Mother was a bit too old then to be running about doing impressions, so she just sat and tried to guess what each person was doing.

When our stay in Scotland was over, we headed back to London, and after a few weeks there, we would go down to Walmer Castle, which was one of the Cinque Ports over which the Queen Mother presided as Lord Warden, the first woman to do so. It was a very prestigious title of which former holders included the Duke of Wellingon, W. H. Smith, the former Australian prime minister Sir Robert Menzies and Sir Winston Churchill.

The Cinque Ports were first mentioned in a Royal Charter of 1155 and, in return for certain privileges, were maintained so that ships could be called upon by the Crown in times of trouble. They effectively served as the Navy in the days when England didn't have one, though most were used for piratical operations against French ships. The five original towns that formed these ports were Sandwich, Dover, Hythe, Romney and Hastings.

The Queen Mother went to Walmer Castle every year for a weekend to entertain all the local dignitaries, and this really was heavy-duty entertaining. I used to take my roller-blades down and go skating along the sea front. She loved watching me do this. We spent Friday to Monday down there and would visit various places, such as the Channel Tunnel, town halls, businesses and that sort of thing. One place we visited was Dover Castle and the warden there was Brigadier Vere Hayes, who I was sat next to during dinner.

Before sitting down, Alastair Aird grabbed me and said, 'Don't ask about the lasagne.'

I said, 'What?'

'Don't ask about the lasagne, you know, the incident with the lasagne,' he added.

Then, minutes later, Ralph said, 'Don't ask if we are having lasagne for dinner, whatever you do...'

I was baffled and sat down to eat in some confusion thinking, does he have some kind of irrational fear of lasagne, only to discover later that the Brigadier's wife had sacked their chef over some incident with the lasagne and it was still a very touchy subject.

Walmer Castle was quite hard work; there is no other way to describe it. There were large numbers of people to organise and lots of memorising of names, and this was a big part of the job. I was expected to know the people who came, or get to know them very quickly. Fortunately, I managed it pretty well. But it was tiring having to be on the ball all the time. There were lots of retired military types down there and they took great pleasure in spotting if you did something wrong and wouldn't hesitate to jump in and try to put you right.

But the place itself was lovely. It was older than Birkhall and the Castle of Mey and for ninety-nine per cent of the year was open to the general public, apart from that one weekend when it was closed for the Queen Mother. Again, it was nice to be out of London and this time in a very pretty coastal town rather than a bleak, windswept outcrop of Scotland. The one saving grace with Walmer was that although we did a lot more entertaining and visited various places, everybody got to bed a bit earlier. I say earlier, but it was still around midnight. But it allowed me to get about seven hours sleep before rising at 7.00 in the morning to plan the day and organise trips and try to remember everyone's name. But this was a solo engagement for the Queen Mother and no other Royal ever came down.

The Royal Family did come together at Christmas at Sandringham, apart from Princess Diana who was absent for obvious reasons. They all stayed for an extended festive break that lasted from the middle of December to mid January, and I would then get the whole of January off. Sandringham is an amazing place, a typical Norfolk stately home that lies on very flat, picturesque grounds. It has been the private home of four generations of the Royal Family since they acquired it 150 years ago, but in that time it has witnessed so much, including the deaths of two monarchs, and it was the venue for the first ever Christmas broadcast. It was bought by Albert, Prince of Wales, for £220,000 in February 1862 and boasts over 600 acres of carefully managed woodland and heath. On 19 January 1915 a Zeppelin crossed the North Sea on a raid and dropped several bombs on and around the estate. One of the craters filled with water and was turned into a duck pond. In 1932, King George V started the tradition of the live Christmas broadcast from Sandringham's 'business room' and, in 1957, Queen Elizabeth II made her first televised Christmas Day broadcast from Sandringham's library.

There was no fishing, or hunting, at Sandringham, and only the occasional shooting forays. The picnic lunches were more formal than in Scotland and seemed to go on forever, sometimes past 5.00 pm. In Scotland, it was really a holiday and most guests stayed for a weekend. But at Sandringham, there was none of that and the guests came for lunch from homes nearby and were expected to leave afterwards. This was what gave it its formality. But I liked Sandringham. Aesthetically, it was the best place to stay, and I celebrated a birthday there for which the Queen Mother arranged for a cake to be brought out and she led a rendition of 'Happy Birthday' with while the other guests sang along. These were the main places we stayed when not at Clarence House and the two years I was with her were the longest she had gone – apart from the War, of course – without travelling abroad.

There were day visits to various places in Britain, of course, and a large part of my job was to arrange these trips which the Queen Mother liked to go on at least once a week. Initially, I was briefed by Alastair who would tell me where and when she wanted to go and I would then draw up an outline plan for the trip involving timings and where she needed to be at such a time, all that sort of thing. Then there was the transport to arrange, and finally I would go on a recce, which meant visiting the place and chatting to the people involved to make sure that things such as access, because the Queen Mother had a stick, were all sorted out, and that the people meant to be meeting her knew what to say and what to do. I would make sure that they were stocked up with gin – Gordon's preferably, because that was what she drank at that time. Plus, I would ensure they had a stock of Dubonnet and knew how to mix her drink. At all the recces I would say to the organisers, 'Just imagine your MD is coming to visit. Just do as you would do with them, only remember to be a little bit more polite because this is the Queen Mother.'

Another thing I had to do was to make sure that the Queen Mother had a seat wherever she was visiting and that it was comfortable. I used to say, 'Don't grab hold of her arm while she walks to her seat and under no circumstances let any of your staff grab hold of her arm if they feel they need to keep her steady on her feet. She'll grab hold of you if she needs to.' But obviously, on the day, people did get into the swing of things and were very, very polite. No one ever behaved inappropriately with her or said anything out of place. But the whole point of the recce was to stop people freaking out and being nervous on the Queen Mother's arrival because she really didn't like that, and she also didn't like to feel a big fuss was being made. If things didn't go to plan or broke down, she would just say, 'Oh well, that is the way it goes,' and leave it at that.

I remember being with her at an Irish Guards bash when one of the poles of the tent we were in fell down and half the canopy collapsed. Fortunately, it wasn't in our half of the tent. She just laughed as she watched the guests getting caught up in the tarpaulin and said, 'Oh well, never mind.'

But you should have seen the look of horror in the officers' eyes. I would hate to have been the poor bugger who put the thing up. He really was for the high jump when she left. But as far as she was concerned it was just a case of 'There you go, these things happen, don't they?'

After a recce, I would go back to the private secretary together with whom I would draw up an outline plan for the visit and distribute this to whoever needed it; so, for example, the drivers would get one instructing them when to be ready and where they needed to go. Then I would brief the Queen Mother on what the timings were for the trip and she would either make slight alterations or, more often than not, go with what I had briefed her on. If the occasion were a military one, I would be in uniform, otherwise I would wear a suit. In the hours leading up to the visit, I liaised closely with security to make sure that everything was in place. For most of these visits, I acted as a sort of official problem solver. I would make sure that everything ran smoothly and that the people meeting the Queen Mother knew how to address her and that sort of thing. Sometimes, though, I really had to sit down with them because they just didn't understand things; these were mainly non-military types who had never been exposed to such a level of protocol before. I had to ram the procedure home and go over it again and again until I thought I was going to throttle them. It was easy with ex-Army types because they addressed her as they would a senior officer.

A good example of a mixed bag of people was the annual Sandringham Flower Show. I would talk to people who had never met royalty before and teach them how to curtsey, much to the amusement of onlookers. Then, during the event, I had to make sure that people knew when to leave. The Sandringham show wasn't orchestrated for her, so she would just go with the flow until I said to her, 'I think we need to be getting off soon, ma'am.' She would simply reply, 'Yes, I think that would be best.'

Historically, she always went to the flower show and she really enjoyed it; it was one of her favourite events, possibly second only to the Cheltenham races. She would laugh and joke with the people she met there, and I don't necessarily think it was because she was interested in the flowers, it was more the people she actually met. I found it quite difficult because I had to meet lots of people I had never met before and make chit-chat. I got a very good idea of what it was like to be a member of the Royal Family and have to ask people meaningful questions all the time without being dull or repetitive. It's actually quite hard to meet hundreds of people and find something different and interesting to say to each of them. Most of the people I met at the show wanted to hand the Queen Mother a gift, flowers mainly. These I would give to the lady-in-waiting who would put them in a car to be taken back to Sandringham where we stayed for the duration of the show.

Fortunately, the pace of life at Sandringham was a little less hectic than at Birkhall, and not as many guests were invited, so I didn't have to stay up until the early hours of the morning. The Queen and Princess Margaret would sometimes pop in but they didn't stay up late. They would do a jigsaw, read the papers and then pop off to bed. I often found I could be fast asleep well before midnight, and the bedroom I stayed in was just fabulous. It was a huge room containing an old mahogany bed with a duck-down mattress, deep shag-pile carpets, great works of art on the wall, mainly from the Impressionist era, and a bathroom with a big Victorian sink finished with lovely brass taps. It was great to stay there.

When it was time to go back to Clarence House, I would follow up on any instructions I had received from the various visits we had been on. Some people asked for a signed photograph or a letter, so I made a note of the people the Queen Mother spoke to and that sort of thing and sent on thank-you notes and other requests. There were two types of thank-you notes: one was from me and the other was from me on behalf of the Queen Mother, and I started the latter with: 'Her Majesty has commanded me to write and thank you for a fabulous day…'

The Queen Mother never wrote any thank-you notes to the public herself; they always followed this pattern. On the other hand, when going on visits, most people would imagine that she followed a set pattern when talking to those she met, that she would have the same set questions which she trotted out time and time again. Well, that wasn't the case at all. When she went to decommission the *Ark Royal*, I remember her asking one sailor, 'How many countries have you visited? Have you been to India?' That was one of her few regrets, that she never visited what was, in her time as Queen Consort, the jewel in Britain's golden Empire.

She said to one sailor, 'You're quite young. I bet you haven't served with this carrier very long?' before listening to virtually his whole life story, which the young chap loved recounting to her as he swelled with pride.

Her questions were geared towards each individual and she always asked the right thing. That was what she was good at. She would ask appropriate but different questions for each trip she went on and talked to people in an easy way. It seemed effortless. On one trip to an RAF base, she spotted a plane and, pointing to it, said to one of the officers lined up to meet her, 'I remember flying in one of those thirty years ago,' and proceeded to give an exact description of where, when and why she flew in one.

Her memory was staggering and you could see she amazed a lot of people with her accuracy for detail and how in tune she was with life in general. Her most popular places to visit by far were places with country houses and nice gardens. She loved walking in wild gardens, going through mazes and admiring huge flower beds, fountains and such like, and she enjoyed hearing about the history of places and finding out who had lived in them and when they were built. Indoor events were mainly confined to military affairs. These she also loved because it meant she could be with 'my boys', as she sometimes affectionately referred to them.

I remember the Queen Mother was in her element at a book club launch at the RAF Club in London. A buffet lunch had been put on and she just walked round the place for a good hour talking to the people about flying and combat missions and just having the time of her life. She was the centre of attention and really took the place by storm. Apart from the flower show and her visit to Walmer Castle, all the events laid on for her were almost entirely military affairs. She would be there when regiments were getting their new colours and that sort of thing. What she didn't like was events where she had to walk around a lot, because, until her hip replacement, she wasn't very mobile. That's where the famous golf buggy came in at the flower show. She really loved that and thought the idea, which was the Queen's, was inspired. It became as synonymous with her as the Popemobile did with Pope John Paul II. She loved her buggy because it was so nippy. And seeing her whizzing about in it with a big smile on her face always got a good reaction from the gathering crowd. The way she was so positive about everything, even in darkest adversity, made me realise that life was about looking on the bright side and I have never forgotten this.

CHAPTER ELEVEN

'GO ON, GO ON, HIT HIM, GO ON, PUNCH HIM!'

It was Scotland and Birkhall. The evening meal had finished and we were all in the sitting room watching television. There were about a dozen of us – the home team and a couple of guests. 'Let's watch an episode of *Keeping Up Appearances*,' the Queen Mother said.

'Certainly, ma'am,' I said, and got the tape, put it in the video recorder and set it to rewind. As I did this, I turned the television on and was horrified to see two boxers slugging it out. They really were beating the living daylights out of each other.

'Oh, I'm sorry about this, ma'am,' I said, fearing that she would recoil at being presented with something as violent and bloody as this, 'Let me turn the television off until the tape has rewound.'

'No, no,' she said. 'Leave this on, Colin, you must leave this on.'

And she insisted on watching the whole bout. Everyone was looking at each other with slightly raised eyebrows as this extraordinary scene unfolded. The Queen Mother, as she became more and more engrossed in the fight, slowly edged herself forwards in her seat and began shouting, 'Go on, hit him again, hit him again... Look, he's going to get up from that... go on, punch him... Oh, he's not going to get up from that.'

She became totally animated. I don't think I ever saw her come to life as much as in that moment when the boxing came on. She was totally engrossed in the fight and oblivious to the other people in the room. At one stage, she even started throwing her own little punches as she urged the boxers on. It was amazing to see her jabbing the air with her hands clenched into little fists and saying, 'Come on, hit him again, hit him again. Come on, come on.'

So I kept it on and we ended up watching the whole fight. It was a good one as well, and at the end of it she said, 'Oh, marvellous. Wasn't that a brilliant fight?'

I just thought, well, this is a new one on me.

Sport did play quite a large part in her life, and when I say 'sport', I mainly mean horse racing. She had been involved in racing since the 1950s and was passionate about it. She was very involved in her own breeding programme and when she turned 100 in August 2000 she had ten horses in training, six brood mares and fifteen young horses that were yet to be raced. And this was a drastically scaled down operation to what it once was. Overall, she had enjoyed 449 wins as an owner over the flat and jumps and annually made about ten trips to the races, health permitting. She loved going to the races. I could see that in her demeanour even before we had set off because she would be slightly chattier, with a glint of excitement in her eye.

One of her favourite visitors to Clarence House was the champion jockey turned mystery writer, Dick Francis. It was he who rode her horse Devon Loch in the 1956 Grand National when the horse, which was leading the race, slipped and collapsed flat on his stomach only 40 yards from the finish line. He came for lunch regularly, every couple of months, and loved to bring a signed copy of a new book he had just written, which, come to think of it, was the only fiction that I ever saw her read. The Queen Mother really was very fond of anything to do with horses, so Dick Francis was quite a big part of her world and had been for a few decades. It was the same when Princess Anne made her occasional visit. Although Anne was into eventing and not racing, they still shared this common bond and horses were the main topic of conversation between them. The Queen Mother's love of racing came about when she was persuaded to buy a horse in the 1950s. She became hooked after that. At Clarence House she would try to have the horse racing on the television whenever she could, and if she couldn't watch a race but had one of her horses running in it, she would make sure that a message was relayed to her as to how it had done.

During my time there, she limited her race trips to Cheltenham and Royal Ascot. On the morning of the Cheltenham Gold Cup, we would all set off from Royal Lodge to be there for about 11.00 and the Queen Mother spent about half a day there before returning to Windsor. This was much longer than she would stay when visiting Army barracks or factories, when the whole thing could, and very often would be, over in a couple of hours. At Cheltenham, she eschewed all distractions, including alcohol; she didn't really drink at the races. She might have one or two glasses of wine with her meal but that was it. She could hardly concentrate on anything else but the racing and when they were running she became totally transfixed. Between races, she would be off talking to the jockeys and the trainers and would potter about the paddock just chatting to whoever was there. It was so lovely and she really enjoyed the informality. Racing and her holiday in Scotland were the two places where she really relaxed.

On Gold Cup day, it was my job to make sure that all the transport was arranged for getting there and back, and once we had arrived, I had to make sure that anyone meeting her was who they said they were and generally that the Queen Mother was okay, which wasn't hard because she was loving every minute of it. But once inside Cheltenham, her racing manager, Piers van Goff, took over, which was fair enough because, as far as horse racing was concerned, I could write what I knew about it on my little finger, so I was of very little use when the Queen Mother wanted to talk shop. I would just toddle off and put bets on. It was a good day out because I was in the Royal Enclosure and had a special pass that got me into every part of the course. So I would spend a lot of time in the enclosures where the trainers hung out, getting tips from them before rushing off to place a bet. The first time I went to Cheltenham, I took £50. I walked out of the place five hours later with over six times that amount and a big smile on my face.

In between my pottering about the racetrack, there was a sit-down lunch that the Queen Mother had to fit in. She regarded it as a bit of a distraction. She wanted to see the horses, not eat. But, fortunately, it was a very informal three-course meal. I say informal because there was a row of television screens in the room relaying all sorts of information about the horses and the odds for the upcoming race. I could tell that the Queen Mother would rather watch the screens than have to chat, but chat she did with about forty guests before getting down to the business of racing again. The whole meal was so casual that you would hardly know a Royal was present if you happened accidentally to walk into the room. The Queen Mother never betted because she never carried money with her, but that is not to say she didn't have people who bet on her behalf. Fortunately, it wasn't me. I didn't know my accumulators from my each ways and would have been sure to cock it up. I would probably have put the money on the wrong horse. When I did tell her about my little windfall, she got very excited for me and clapped her hands together and said, 'Well done, Colin.'

I had a lot of conversations with her about horse racing;

they mainly involved her instructing me in the intricacies of it. I remember her telling me the difference between flat racing and the jumps. She said, 'The more expensive horses race over the flat so there's a little bit more prestige about flat racing than there is about jump racing.' She added, 'It's much harder to train up a young horse to be a successful flat racer than over the jumps, but if you want to get into the business, I would advise that you buy a horse which races over the jumps because they are a lot cheaper and you've got more chance of success.'

I had, and still have, no intention of ever buying a horse. Even if I could afford one! But I valued her know-how and her inexhaustible knowledge of individual horses, their trainers, owners and form. She really did know the business inside out and took calls almost every day on some aspect of horse racing. But to be honest, it really wasn't my bag at all. I thought places like Cheltenham were interesting up to a point, but once I had experienced it, I was happy not to go back for another three or four months and I certainly wouldn't choose to go to the races in my free time. But fair play to the Queen Mother, who tried to educate me in the ways of horse racing and to convert me to her way of thinking. She would tell me which horses preferred soft ground and which hard, those who had just recovered from an injury, all sorts of information. But I'm afraid I found it very hard to stop my eyes from glazing over. And trips to Royal Ascot, the other big occasion in the racing calendar, weren't really for the Queen Mother, even though the whole thing was more prestigious. In the social calendar,

Royal Ascot is much bigger than Cheltenham and this was the crux of the problem as far as the Queen Mother was concerned. It was, and still is, seen as more of a social event than a race meeting and people go to be seen rather than to concentrate on the horses. It's like watching a Formula One rally in Europe; you could be watching it in a whole host of different countries, but if you go to the Monaco Grand Prix, it's totally different to anywhere else. People go there to be seen; they are not really interested in the motor racing. And the same sort of thing happens at Ascot. The Queen Mother really didn't enjoy Ascot as much as she enjoyed Cheltenham, which was much more personal because the people there belonged to a more hardcore horse racing set and they really knew about horses, more so than the people who visited Royal Ascot. I would say that eight out of ten of the women who went to Royal Ascot were more bothered about the hat they were wearing and whether it was different from anyone else's than who was running in the 2.15. The Queen Mother couldn't stand all that superficial nonsense. But she would go and she would enjoy it to a point. It's like the difference between those who attend church at Christmas and those who go regularly on a Sunday. Ascot was filled with Christmas church people who just wanted to be seen at the races once a year – but Cheltenham is full of the real churchgoers and there is an almost spiritual feeling towards racing.

I found Ascot to be filled with very pompous, snotty and arrogant people, the only saving grace being that the Queen Mother was not like that so I found myself in this hilarious situation where people would talk to me in a very aloof and standoffish manner until they found out who I represented and then their whole demeanour completely changed and they would be at their most charming. It really was ridiculous and the Queen Mother didn't enjoy Ascot because of this and preferred Cheltenham because it was much more intimate and she could sit in a box, watch the race in peace and just generally get a bit of space. Ascot was filled with Elizabeth Arden beauticians, bankers and Essex girls wearing silly hats and short skirts. The Queen Mother was very protective of her love of horses and preferred to be surrounded by people who cared about the sport, so one can imagine her reaction to everything that went on at Ascot. At Cheltenham when she walked into a paddock there was a general round of applause, whereas at Ascot you'd have whooping and cheering as though she was some kind of B-list celebrity. It was clear from her body language that she just wasn't 100 per cent happy with the Ascot scene. She just wanted to see the horses but ended up being fussed over.

The difference between Ascot and Cheltenham very much reflected the Queen Mother's own personality. She liked things for a reason rather than being seen to like the right things, and in this respect she prided herself on not being politically correct. She'd say things to me like: 'That is not very PC, but then again I'm not a very PC person.' If you didn't like someone or something, she would much rather you said you didn't like it and tell it the way it was, rather than hide behind some politically correct view. She appreciated people being straight, even though, in her role, she couldn't really give an opinion.

Personally, I preferred Cheltenham because at Ascot the security was much tighter. There were a lot more people milling around so the police enforced much tighter restrictions on things like passes. It just wasn't as easy to get around the place. The security staff would be on the lookout for all sorts of people, from celebrity stalkers to terrorist bombers, whereas at Cheltenham, you could just feel and see the police – who were happier being there because the crowd was there for the racing and nothing more. The overall atmosphere at Ascot was hugely different to Cheltenham; it was much more formal and I hate anything with too much formality. Ascot was also filled with people pretending to be something they weren't. It was all a little bit 'chavvy' before the term 'chav' had even been invented.

The Queen Mother spent much less time at Ascot than she did at Cheltenham, maybe two or three hours at the most. It was just a quick in and out in the afternoon. Once there, she would try to watch the racing, but there were so many people there wanting to see and be seen with her that she just didn't get a chance to watch anything. Imagine going to a football match and someone constantly talking to you all the way through so you miss the game. That was what Ascot was like for the Queen Mother. She once said to me, 'Cheltenham is so much more about the horses and Ascot is more about the people who go.' But it was required of her to go to Royal Ascot because her attendance had become something of a tradition.

Obviously, other members of the Royal Family also went to Ascot. The Queen also shares a love of horses and would talk racing and form with the Queen Mother quite often. She would ask her mother how one of her horses had raced in the 2.15 at York or something like that, and they would talk about particular horses, injuries, riders, and so on. A lot of it was lost on me and I would just switch off. The Queen Mother didn't really study form in the newspapers; she didn't subscribe to *Sporting Life* or the *Racing Post*, but then again she didn't need to. If she wanted any information on any horse, she just rang Michael Oswald who ran her studs and kept her fully informed of everything. People joked about how the Queen Mother used to have a racing results tickertape machine in one of the upstairs rooms at Clarence House, but that was not the case. She could get the result of any race, or any information on any horse or jockey, just by picking up the phone.

The Queen Mother did have other sports she enjoyed: drag hunting, where schoolboy cross-country runners are chased by hounds as a way of introducing them to the delights of hunting with dogs; rowing – she made sure she never missed the Oxford and Cambridge boat race on television; tennis – I remember after she watched one particularly memorable Wimbledon tie she said to me, 'Oh, Jeremy Bates is in good form'; and, to a lesser degree, she enjoyed cricket. She was very aware at that time how bad England's cricket team was.

But nothing took the place of horse racing; no other sport came close. Her love of racing also rubbed off on her staff, who were all quite knowledgeable, mainly because they had been listening to her. But the only person I know who shared her boundless enthusiasm for it was one of her secretaries, Fiona Fletcher, who loved her horses with a passion. But it didn't do anything for her career prospects because as far as the Queen Mother was concerned, she was a secretary and secretaries didn't really get close enough to members of the Royal Family for intimate chats. That was the exclusive preserve of the home team.

One thing the Queen Mother did miss out on which I think she would have loved was the so-called extreme sports that were just catching on at that time. Things like snowboarding were in their infancy while other sports such as white water rafting were beginning to make the breakthrough on programmes such as *Grandstand*. She would have loved these sports. I say that because she enjoyed the idea of fast cars and motorbikes and took a huge interest in the fact that I came to work every morning on my 600cc motorbike, as opposed to Ralph who would look at me dressed in my leathers with disdain in his eyes and say, 'I see you're dressed in your Man From Mars outfit.'

He couldn't understand why I didn't wear a white scarf and goggles because that is what he would have worn. But the Queen Mother was very taken by my motorbike, mainly because no other equerry had ever ridden in to work on a motorbike before. It did raise eyebrows among other, more stuffy members of staff. But I thought it was fun and the Queen Mother thought it was fabulous. She'd say things to me like, 'Oh, Colin, I would love to have a go on your bike.

Why don't you bring it into the garden and we can ride round on it!'

So one morning, I brought my bike into the garden of Clarence House and her eyes lit up when she saw it, although she did say to me, 'I think perhaps it's a little too big for me to ride, but you have a go, Colin.'

I rode round on my motorbike making a huge din and she was so impressed that, at one stage, she clapped her hands together and said, 'Oh my life, what a wonderfully big thing it is.'

She loved gadgets, gizmos and boys' toys anyway. There is a story about the Princes William and Harry showing her how to play on their PlayStation console and I can fully believe that because it really would be something she would have enjoyed. I remember one guest talking about windsurfing and her being rapt as he described everything about it. She would have loved the whole concept of going windsurfing and biking, and I think if I had turned up in her garden on a smaller Maserati, she would have sat on it and may even have had a go, although Alastair probably would have tried to put a stop to it. It was the same with soft-top sports cars. Anyone who turned up at Clarence House in a soft-top sports car could guarantee that within half an hour of them arriving they would be back out on the road and driving round with the Queen Mother inside. Alternatively, she would ask so many questions about the car that one couldn't avoid saying the inevitable, 'Would you like me to take you for a spin?'

She was so into flash cars and loved going for a drive in

Viscount Linley's cars. No one ever recognised her as they drove round the streets of London for two reasons: no one has ever really seen the Queen Mother in a headscarf, and because you would never expect to see a woman in her nineties haring through the streets of London in a top-of-the-range sports car. She thought it very daring to go out in disguise. But she really didn't want to be recognised; she just liked the feel of being in a sports car and wanted to escape for a bit. I remember one time up in Scotland, when I drove her about in a Range Rover with a long wheelbase on Sundays when chauffeurs got the day off. We were on our way to church and suddenly she said, 'Come on, Colin, let's open her up a bit.'

I thought that I had better be careful because I was terrified of crashing the car or bumping into something. It wasn't that I'm a bad driver, it was just that when you have a passenger as important as the Queen Mother sitting next to you it does make you slightly self-conscious about what you are doing. But she was all for it, saying, 'Come on Colin, put your foot down.' So I did, but she kept on saying, 'Colin, why can't we go any faster?'

She liked to feel a bit of speed under her feet and that's why I think she would have adored extreme sports. If there is such a thing as reincarnation then she will probably come back as a snowboarder.

CHAPTER TWELVE

'GET YOUR BLACK TIE ON BECAUSE ONE OF THE GUESTS HAS DIED'

The Queen Mother never really went in for the kind of grandiose State banquets that the Queen regularly put on for visiting foreign dignitaries at Buckingham Palace. By 1994, all her dining arrangements took place at much smaller venues and normally at a function of her choosing. Most of her meals away from the regular places were at Army and Navy dinners or similar events. I went with her to many of them and they were good bashes. Everybody she met was so incredibly pleased to see her and she would never fail to give people what they were looking for and a bit more. Sometimes I would get a call before her arrival from some public relations chap who would say, 'Would the Queen Mother like a blanket to keep her warm?'

To which I replied, 'No, but you had better check that the regimental colonel knows his stuff about the history of the regiment and their deployments over the next few years because the Queen Mother will almost certainly ask about them.'

There would be a stunned silence before he said, 'Oh, yes, I'm sure he does, but I had better check anyway.'

I remember a Red Arrows function at the RAF Club in London to which the Queen Mother was invited as the Arrows' honorary colonel, and one of the officers rang me to ask if there were any special requirements.

'No,' I said, 'But if I were you, I would be prepared to answer some very specific questions about operations, as the Queen Mother will ask you.'

Again, there was a silence, before he said, 'Oh, right, right ho, will do.'

I'm sure some people I spoke to thought she was a frail old lady who was starting to lose her marbles because some of them would say, 'Oh, come on, she can't be that with it,' when I told them what she was like.

I could tell they were wondering, how alert can a ninety-plus-year-old woman be? When they met her, they realised she was a live-wire. But she did shun the big events that the Queen had to attend. It was more a case of big things being done for her, rather than her attending big events. But that's not to say that I didn't have to go to these big bashes at Buckingham Palace. Sometimes, I would be at home in my flat and I would get a call from Toby Williamson, the Queen's equerry, almost frantic, saying, 'What are you doing tonight?'

'Why, what's the problem?' I would say.

And he would tell me that a guest had gone down with

flu, or that their car had broken down, or even that they had died – it really could be anything – and then he would add, 'Could you get yourself over here as quickly as possible because we need to make up the numbers.'

If a guest dropped out of any dinner with the Queen, it was a headache because there would be immediate problems with things like the table placement as there would be an odd one out. So the Queen's staff phoned up other members of the Royal Household to make up the numbers. This happened about once or twice a week and I don't think I ever turned them down, which is probably why they called me so often, come to think of it. You couldn't really say no to the Queen. What were the chances of anyone having a commitment more important than dinner with the Queen of the United Kingdom? I always said yes, and if I had anything else planned I just dropped it. Sometimes, I would be given two or three hours' notice; at other times it was twenty minutes, and I always had a black tie and dinner jacket on hand for these sorts of eventualities. I would just whip them on and walk across Green Park to the Palace all dolled up and feeling a bit like James Bond. Once at the palace, I assumed a role as part of the team on hand to entertain the guests. This meant mingling with the assembled party and making sure that they felt comfortable and had a drink to hand. It wasn't just a case of getting me in to make up the numbers. Once there, I was seen as a member of staff who actually had to chip in.

The banquets would start between 7.00 and 7.30 in the evening and go on for about three hours. Again, they were quite boozy bashes, like any dinner party, really. But the whole feel of the place was totally different from Clarence House. Buckingham Palace was bigger, less personal and more akin to a big corporation rather than someone's home. There were something like twenty times the number of staff that were at Clarence House, and I never got to know who many of the less senior staff such as the butlers were. There was quite a rapid changeover of personnel at the Palace and that gave it the feel of a big business. At Clarence House, I knew who everyone was and we were almost like an extended family to the Queen Mother.

My opposite number, Toby, had a much more formal role as the Queen's equerry and unlike me rarely saw his boss other than to brief her for about an hour a day. His was a more functional job as opposed to mine, which was semi-social. He came from a Navy background and was very formal. He worked on a grand stage and became slightly detached from real life, despite the fact that he was the same age as me and as a lieutenant commander in the Navy had an equivalent rank to mine. We were almost contemporaries. His job, although bigger than mine in terms of position, was more straightforward because it had a set routine and there were more staff on hand to whom he could delegate matters and whom he could call on for advice.

The Queen relied much more on her private secretary. He effectively ran the whole show at Buckingham Palace and had a much bigger impact on the Queen's life than her equerry did. Toby was relied on to organise military functions and was seen primarily as an events organiser. If you had to compare him with me, I would say we were the same size fish but his was a much bigger pond. To some degree, I could have done his job and to the same degree, he couldn't have done mine.

A lot of Palace employees said I had the best job in London and looking back, reflecting on the endless gin and tonics I poured out from the huge walk-in drinks cupboard, and all the schmoozing with leggy blondes, and meeting poets and war heroes and artists, I suppose I did. Toby was certainly more stressed than I was. But he had more to do because the Queen, being who she is, was much busier. After all, how many State functions did the Queen Mother go to? I can tell you: none, and I was glad I worked for her because it meant I did have some social life after work. With the Queen there was a vast number of evening functions that Toby was required to attend and so he didn't really have any life at all. He was at the Palace virtually the whole time and it took it out of him.

But if being the Queen's equerry was more stressful than being the Queen Mother's, it was nothing compared to working for Prince Charles and his then estranged wife, Princess Diana. Working for those two meant you were in the eye of a particularly nasty hurricane.

The Prince of Wales's equerry undertook a very similar role to the Queen's. It was very functional and much more like that of an events co-ordinator and manager. But it was given a much more complex dimension when Charles and Diana split because their separation polarised the staff, who had no choice but to take sides. They were either with

Charles and against Diana or vice versa, and that made things extremely difficult. Diana took some staff to Kensington Palace and Charles kept the rest. It really was rather dramatic, but it was pretty obvious to the staff who were watching all this unfold from the sidelines who would go where. People like Paul Burrell had always served Diana, so it was an easy choice for him to make, as it was for their respective valets and maids. But it did cause some awful tensions among opposing staff members.

People like Ralph and Alastair, who were very much old-school servants, were horrified by what was going on. It was just extraordinary to them that the salacious details of the Waleses' marriage breakdown should be dragged through the tabloid press and debated on television. They thought it bizarre. But they reserved a fierce loyalty and some sympathy for Charles, simply because he was such a nice man and also because they realised that without him the whole Monarchy could come crumbling down in some sort of Republican revolt. Ralph was 100 per cent loyal to the Crown and that was that. He was terribly upset when Charles and Diana went on television to have a pop at each other; it gave him palpitations. The poor man was almost reduced to tears. And it also upset Charles' equerry, who was extremely stressed out most of the time because the whole break-up affected the staff as well as the warring couple. It was a very difficult position to be in. All the staff struggled because there were a lot of weird things going on and a great deal of distrust between the various personalities who were competing for either Charles' or Diana's affections. No one really knew where certain people's loyalties lay, and the ones who did nail their colours to the mast, like Charles' valet Michael Fawcett, could be an absolute bloody nightmare to work for.

Fawcett sided with Charles all the way and when I first met him, I had no idea he had the power that he had. I could never quite work out how a simple valet could rise to this level of authority, because within the Royal Household his was really quite a minor job. He would get the Prince up in the morning and dressed, make sure his suits were ironed and his uniforms correct and that he was well turned out and in effect that was that. But he had somehow managed, with the trust and full knowledge and co-operation of the Prince, to build up a huge power base which threatened the whole employee structure within St James's Palace. Other people knew how powerful he was, and I was intrigued because, when I saw him for the first time, I had done something to upset him – I think I had left a ghillie waiting – and he snapped at me, 'You shouldn't leave a ghillie waiting.'

I responded in the politest way possible with, 'And who are you?'

'I'm Michael Fawcett,' he answered.

'Who?' I said.

'I'm the valet,' he added.

'Well,' I said, 'If I want my shirts pressed, I'll let you know right away.'

Other members of Charles' staff who were in the room witnessed all this and I could sense the sucking in of cheeks as they viewed the confrontation with horror. As I looked around, I could tell they were thinking, you can't talk to him like that. But I thought, no way will I be spoken to like that by a member of staff whose job is to press shirts. Fortunately, our paths never really crossed after that and because our jobs were so far removed, he never became a problem for me. But Fawcett was like this with all the staff. He was rude, brusque and acted in a manner that was very much above his station. Eventually, in 1998, he was kicked out when almost every single member of staff simultaneously complained about him. It was a coup of monumental proportions. He would shout and scream at them when it wasn't his place to do so. Although there were also rumours that he sold unwanted royal gifts for cash, a claim he always strongly denied. But one thing is for certain, he very much had the Prince's ear, more so than any other member of staff and when he was booted out he was given a lucrative new job as a personal consultant to Charles on a handsome six-figure salary with a house worth half a million pounds thrown in for good measure. Later, when a probe into the various scandals surrounding the Prince's office was due to be published, Fawcett was offered an equally lucrative job with his boss's favourite catering company, a £100,000-a-year role at the society party organisers The Admirable Crichton, again with a house thrown in for good measure. I was outraged. My former wife worked as an assistant to Prince Charles and when she got on the wrong side of Fawcett, he would scream and rant at her and almost reduced her to tears.

He was quite simply a nightmare, and that was a good

description of how it was to work for the Prince at that time. If you walked into one of Charles' offices any time between 1994 and 1996, you could easily witness something being thrown at someone in anger. Whether it was a pen, a book or a paperweight, it would be picked up and hurled. Even the Prince would pick things up and launch them at one of his staff if that person had done something wrong, or said something inappropriate to the press. It was mainly the butlers who had things thrown at them; they bore the brunt of most of the problems. But Charles' staff could cope with his occasional bouts of bad temper because he really was living on the edge – Diana's leaks to the press about his private life were driving him to despair. They could cope because they also saw a much more positive side to him. He had energy, he was full of life and generally interested in people, so for ninety per cent of the time he was lovely to work for. He was chatty and very personable. But he was also supremely creative and massively intelligent and that came at a price. The Prince did have a dark side that manifested itself in a short temper. I think you find this in most creative and artistic types. So his staff tolerated his outbursts. What they couldn't put up with was Fawcett. But this didn't bother the valet in the slightest. So long as he had Charles behind him he was happy. But Charles had other things to worry about than the shenanigans of certain members of his staff. His personnel was huge and he was rather like the chief executive of a large company who wouldn't know what every employee was up to; similarly, Charles didn't know what all his staff were doing all the time. I would never have worked for Prince Charles, not for double the money I was on at Clarence House. St James's Palace was so political it was a minefield. Prince Charles was surrounded by one or two bad eggs. My world was a happy place.

Working for Princess Diana at Kensington Palace was equally fraught. She was so temperamental at that time and you experienced the full spectrum of her emotions because she was so very changeable and moody. One minute, she would be up, the next down. The biggest problem for her staff was dealing with what I would term her moments of extreme behaviour when she would do things like go off into London alone without her bodyguards or any member of staff to accompany her. She did this quite regularly, sparking mass panic among those back at Kensington Palace, who would launch a hunt to try and find her. I remember one of the Queen Mother's chauffeurs driving along Sloane Street and, quite by chance, he spotted Diana on her own trying to cross the road. He pulled over and said, 'Ma'am, jump in now,' and in she hopped to be taken back to the palace.

It was absolute madness because she was a target for everyone from lone stalkers to complete nutters – and, believe me, she attracted a hell of a lot of those – to groups such as the IRA and other terrorists. And she always chose to go out alone during the day at the busiest times; sometimes she would be in disguise, but the disguises she chose were not very effective. This put unimaginable pressure on her security staff who knew that they would have taken the blame if anything had happened to her.

At Kensington Palace, she did have an equerry, but he had the job from hell because Diana was on the verge of a complete breakdown. She telephoned the wives of certain members of her own staff and insinuated that their husband was having an affair and made all sorts of wild accusations, such as: 'Do you know where your husband was last night?'

It was all totally unfounded and all the product of Diana's imagination. She would make these calls at all times of the day and night and her equerry was forced to pick up the pieces until eventually he could take no more and left. He was one of the most stressed people I met in the royal employ. He was, after all, working for someone who had become totally unhinged mentally and in some respects was quite dangerous. As the media began to smell blood around Charles and Diana's failing marriage, so Diana began to rely more and more on her core staff for emotional support and guidance. But she expected some emotional commitment in return; in fact, she demanded it. Some, like her butler Paul Burrell, did give her their support; others didn't. But she could be capricious in the way she treated members of staff. Paul Burrell may have described himself as her rock, but I'm sure the feeling wasn't reciprocated by Diana, because as soon as she thought a member of staff was getting too close to her emotionally, she simply threw down the shutters. She was far too complex and by no means a simple black and white character. Certain members of staff would find they were flavour of the month one minute and completely off her radar the next. Victoria Mendem was a good example. She was one of Diana's secretaries who spent a lot of time organising her social diary. Sometimes Diana would take her on holiday with her and pay for everything, other times she would be a bit off with her. It all depended on what her mood was at the time.

Working for Charles and Diana was a constant strain, and it didn't suit fragile characters such as George Smith, who was a former footman and valet to Charles. He had served as a soldier in the Welsh Guards during the 1980s and fought in the Falklands War and in Northern Ireland. That experience together with the drama of Charles' and Diana's problems and the fact his marriage broke down meant that it was no surprise when midway through my stint as equerry, he started having the most horrendous nightmares and flashbacks to the bombing of HMS *Sir Galahad*, the Royal Navy ship on which he served during the Falklands conflict. To ease these problems, he hit the bottle in a big way, which made things a hell of a lot worse. I saw him occasionally and he would very often be bleary-eyed and look drawn and tired, but he was a lovely man, and it was such a shame to see his spiralling decline. He was the physical manifestation of Charles and Diana's marriage and when they split, he was one of the few people to get caught in the middle.

Initially, he sided with Charles, but Diana really liked him and thought he was very nice and that his problems could be sorted out. She felt for him and took him under her wing. Eventually, he ended up doing some driving for her – a little risky considering his problems with alcohol, but there you go. Now this did rattle the Prince of Wales a bit and Diana enjoyed that fact, but she did care for the man, although he was being used as a pawn between them. It was a bit odd to see them fighting over possession of this wreck of a man. Maybe they saw all their problems through him, I don't know. But it got to the point where Charles intervened and got him into the Priory and took a personal interest in making sure he got better, which is a very royal trait. They do help people when they are down, as the Queen Mother proved with Ralph. But I think George got to the point where he was beyond help. He really had reached the end of the long dark tunnel and could see nothing for himself on the other side.

My then girlfriend, Lizzie, who was the Prince of Wales' assistant personnel officer, also stepped in to help on Charles' behalf and took him to a cottage on the Highgrove estate to recuperate. But this only made matters worse because, while there, he alleged that he had been raped by a senior member of staff. He repeated these allegations to Diana who then leaked them to the press. He had already made claims to the police that he was being followed, that threats were being made against him and that strangers were banging on his front door. But when the police set up CCTV cameras outside his home to verify this and he continued to make the same allegations despite video-taped evidence which showed that no one was following him or banging on his door, they approached the Prince's staff and warned him unless George received urgent help, he would be prosecuted for wasting police time. So he was sent to the Priory, only for Diana to make regular visits on at least four occasions to discuss the rape allegations. After his release, he continued to visit her at Kensington Palace, where Diana taped all their conversations. Ultimately, when the press got hold of these allegations, they hunted him down and the poor man was subjected to all sorts of negative publicity. He was branded a liar and a chancer, which made him even more paranoid than before.

At Clarence House, we followed these events with growing incredulity. I just thought, poor old George, he really doesn't need to be used like this in his current state. He was eventually given a £38,000 pay-off by Charles and ended his life living as a depressed, jobless alcoholic in South Wales with his father. He was eventually sacked from his last job as a theatre assistant at the Royal Gwent Hospital in Newport because he had taken too many days off sick and I firmly believe that this is what did for him in the end, because he died in August 2005 in circumstances that have yet to be revealed. Looking back on his life, I just thank God that I worked for the Queen Mother because working for Charles and Diana really was bad for your health.

With everything that was going on – the fights, Diana's *Panorama* interview and the books and various newspaper stories – it was no surprise to find the Queen Mother a little quieter during these turbulent moments. It was difficult to put your finger on her change in mood, but there definitely was a change in her general demeanour whenever something bad broke. She simple wasn't as effervescent and as bright as she normally was and there were some days when she was much quieter than usual. Generally, she just looked a bit sad when she was upset by something, and the only thing that did upset her at that time was the ongoing crises of Charles and Diana, and Andrew and Fergie. She wouldn't talk about it, nor would she be overtly miserable or short-tempered, but she would be more pensive. The Queen Mother was a very private person in that respect and was not big on showing her feelings. The staff just went about their normal business, knowing full well that there was nothing they could do to bring her out of it. We would have been overstepping the mark if we had tried to cheer her up.

CHAPTER THIRTEEN

'DID YOU GET LUCKY THIS WEEKEND, COLIN?'

I realised once my tenure was nearing its end that it was okay not to be completely at one with the system. I found in the Queen Mother the same sort of maverick streak that ran through me. Mine came mainly through my job as an Army pilot. As a pilot, you do observe the military command structure that's in place, but once you are up in the sky, you are very much your own person making your own decisions and thinking outside the bubble of military protocol. In the Army, on the other hand, where you obey orders and don't really think for yourself and it is up to your commanding officer to make the decisions which you then follow through. I went from flying planes to working for the Queen Mother and discovered very quickly that it was rather like being in the RAF in that the Queen Mother liked to bend the rules to suit a particular occasion and liked others to do so as well. I very quickly found myself chatting away to her and being open and friendly and telling jokes, and she responded very positively to the fact that I was not trying to be someone I wasn't, as a few of her former equerries had been.

I must admit that before I joined, I thought the Queen Mother would be a stickler for formality. Admittedly, where she did tend to follow protocol she also liked to be a bit naughty in her own way and dispense with the conventions when the situation demanded. I realised that in her position she made the rules and wasn't as formal as the majority of people below her in the pecking order. Working at Clarence House made me realise that the more formal a person is, and you couldn't get more formal than the Queen Mother, the more stuffy a place doesn't have to be. There was absolutely no stuffiness about the Queen Mother; it came from the people around her. Other members of the upper classes, what I would term the junior upper classes, are the model of stuffiness. It seems ridiculous. I have seen generals in the Army who were stuffy yet whom I regarded as mavericks, but then when I met the Queen Mother, a real maverick, she just wasn't stuffy at all. I felt that this was the way everybody should run their life and behave. It was how I wanted to run my life. When you were sitting next to the Queen Mother and she said to you, 'Let's do this while no one is looking' or 'Let's sneak away and go somewhere else,' it seemed fun.

It opened the gates for me just to be myself. I acted very differently before and after I worked for the Queen Mother. Pre-Queen Mother, I was much more prone to obeying the system and its rules. Afterwards, there was a gradual deterioration. I wasn't prepared to obey rules and orders if they seemed trivial or ridiculous. In effect, I had given up listening to bullshit. My job had had no hard and fast rules. I remember generals who came to meet the Queen Mother scrutinising what I did and trying to make out exactly what the role of equerry to the Queen Mother was. I viewed it as some form of black art.

The biggest thing I took away with me was the concept that you could just be yourself. I realised it was okay not to worry about whether you were making the right impression. It was fine just to be yourself and not to get too hung up about formality because, if things like protocol got in the way of friendliness, the Queen Mother would always choose to be friendly. If she ever saw someone not talking or being a bit stuffy, she would say: 'Go and introduce yourself to that person over there. You'll like them, they have a fabulous job,' or words to that effect.

And if she felt someone was being ignored or a guest was having a hard time, she would say something or do something to alleviate the problem, and I have taken those lessons on board and added them to my life and I hope they have made me a better person. She has definitely made me more pro-active in my life the Queen Mother was very pro-active. When I was driving her around Scotland during her summer break, she once spotted a gate to a field that was open. There were cows in the field so she said, 'Colin, stop the car, we must close that gate or the cows will escape.'

So I stopped the car, got out and closed the gate. Most

people would take the view that it was the farmer's fault for leaving it open and just drive past. But the Queen Mother wasn't like that and I benefited from these experiences which did impact on my later life and also impacted on other members of the Clarence House staff.

I also took something else away from Clarence House with me – a wife! As I mentioned in a previous chapter, the equerry before me said it was the best place you could ever wish to be to meet women, but the majority of them weren't for me. They were all rather Sloaney types and I didn't go for that kind. Some Army officers I knew thought these women were the business and were in seventh heaven when they met them, and there were lots of them; the place was bursting with young ladies, who to top up their weekly allowance from daddy were working as secretaries. A lot of them did their duties grudgingly and many, who didn't really have to work, came into the Royal Household because they were looking for the right man to marry and their parents had told them that the right sort of person was only to be found at one of the royal residences. And I suppose I must have been the right sort. I was young, single and an Army officer. Whether women found me attractive or not, I wouldn't like to say. What I probably didn't do is cash in on the opportunities I had. Some of my predecessors dated a lot of palace girls. The Queen Mother was quite keen on this. On Monday, she would always ask me if I had 'got lucky' over the weekend but wouldn't really push it any further than 'Was she a nice girl?' if I had.

As far as women went, I preferred those with real, three-dimensional personalities and that probably accounts for the fact that my now ex-wife, Elizabeth, was the only woman I dated who worked at the palace during the two years I was there. I saw her coming in on her motorbike every day, and a girl coming in to work for Prince Charles on a 400cc motorbike and dressed in leathers made me think she had an interesting story. The first time we met was when I spotted her getting off her bike and I just took this as an opportunity to go up to her and say hello. She didn't seem that interested in me at first, so to gain her interest, I rang her up one day when she had earlier fallen off her bike in an accident and damaged her petrol tank. The poor girl had had to push her bike from Hampstead to St James's Palace, so I pretended to be the editor of *What Bike?* magazine. I told her that I was doing an article on how women couldn't control motorbikes and I remember there being a stunned silence on the other end until eventually she realised it was a wind-up and said, 'Look, who is this?'

After that we fixed up a date. It started getting serious when she told a friend of mine, 'I really like Colin.'

But this friend said, 'I wouldn't hold your breath because he's not going to commit to anyone.'

That made me think, well, here's a challenge, and I told her it couldn't be further from the truth. We were married by the Queen's chaplain, William Booth, and he was quite brilliant, possibly the best person I met at Clarence House. He was funny, charming, very genuine and honest. He was the total antithesis of the pompous and snooty types you sometimes found there. A lot of palace staff took a sort of cursory interest in colleagues and were fairly flippant about showing any interest in what they said. This didn't apply to William. He was genuinely interested in people and always had loads of time for you if you needed someone to talk to.

When I told the Queen Mother I was getting married, she was pleased without seeming too bothered. When I told her that my fiancée worked for the Prince of Wales, her eyes suddenly lit up and I could see her mentally ticking the boxes in her head. She quite enjoyed the fact that I hadn't gone for the archetypal Sloaney girl but instead had chosen one who was half African and certainly not the usual palace type. At the time, Elizabeth was the only mixed race girl working there, which caused problems for us later. But the Queen Mother loved that fact, I think mainly because she had fond memories of visiting South Africa after the War, and in terms of race she never really differentiated between black and white people; she treated everyone equally, regardless of race or colour, and she never made a passing joke or smirky comment that could be construed as racist or homophobic. Obviously she did make jibes at the French and Germans, but doesn't everyone? I see that as a quintessential British trait passed down through generations. But the Queen Mother was very positive about my engagement and asked me all sorts of questions which included everything from where we were getting wed to what kind of ring I had got Elizabeth to who the best man was and all the usual things, some of which I couldn't answer because I hadn't even thought about them myself. She really did want to know about every aspect of my life and I couldn't really fob her off with any old answer. I probably ended up telling her more about my life than I had ever told my parents because the Queen Mother could handle anything.

You couldn't shock her, and I knew I could have a frank and open discussion with her about anything, as would Dame Frances Campbell-Preston, who would tell the Queen Mother all about her time manning the Samaritans switchboard. The Queen Mother gave me some good advice on marriage and relationships, though, unfortunately, I didn't really heed it because we were divorced some years later.

Elizabeth's job as assistant personnel officer for Prince Charles was a bit more complex than mine because of the internal politics going on at St James's Palace at that time. Although my job had its moments, it was nothing compared to hers. The Prince had a much larger staff and they were all slightly on edge, especially people like Charles' deputy private secretary Mark Bolland, dubbed his spin doctor, and his private secretary Richard Aylard, who found that they were constantly dragged into press reports, misquoted and all sorts of things. They were quite nervy and constantly feared that their jobs were on the line or that someone was going to report them to the Prince. It all sounded a bit of a nightmare to me, and Liz was definitely under more pressure than I was, but all the staff in Prince Charles' office coped with it because they weren't used to anything else. But everything came to a head in the most horrible and traumatic way when my wife got pregnant. These moments are ones you are supposed to enjoy, but she ended up taking Prince Charles to an industrial tribunal over matters involving racial discrimination and being forced out of her job, and all the while she was coping with the pressures of having a new child. This caused all sorts of problems and was one of the contributing factors to our splitting up. It didn't help that she lost the case by the narrowest of verdicts: a two-to-one majority. One tribunal member went with her, one went with the Prince and the third took a further two hours to deliberate before coming down on the side of Charles. It was a close call, but it left both of us devastated. Basically, Charles' office had accused Liz of not fulfilling her contractual terms. They claimed that she hadn't been doing the sufficient number of hours required of her. Mark Bolland ended up pulling her in off maternity leave and gave her a disciplinary warning. She was told that while she had been pregnant, it was thought that she would have been 'too hormonal' to cope with it. I remember her coming home absolutely incredulous and very, very upset, saying, 'Can you believe what they have just said to me about this?'

The whole episode was deeply harrowing and made worse by the fact that the tribunal was reported extensively in the press in much more detail than I care to go into. Like most people who worked for Charles and at some stage find themselves being dragged into the quagmire of salacious gossip and battles which eventually end up in print, Liz was one of the many victims. She told the tribunal, 'They wanted a white face at Highgrove and I was not that face. In the Prince of Wales' household, there is still very much the old school and they have not really taken to black people. I never felt part of the team. There were always black jokes and names going round. Because it is the Royal Family it is still very protected. It has its own rules and regulations. We are servants. People who work for the Prince of Wales are not employees and to be a servant's servant is bad enough but to be a black servant's servant is worse. I would never have the old school tie and I would never be one of them, even though I did a good job.'

But Charles' equerry Stephen Lamport insisted there was no reason Liz should have felt like this. He told the tribunal: 'There was no wish among anyone in the office to push Lizzie out of her job. She was a valued member of the Prince of Wales' household for a long period of time.'

He then went on to say – and you'll understand the irony in this – 'Highgrove is not managed in a very confrontational way. Loyalty and experience matter a lot. Very rarely do we deal with things through confrontation.'

It came down to Lizzie's word against the establishment's and they were quite prepared to pull together, whatever their differences of opinion and personality clashes might be. She didn't stand a chance, to be honest. But in my opinion, this whole nightmare was not the Prince of Wales' fault. I felt that in his organisation things weren't done properly and situations were mishandled. Lots of people left and were unhappy and Liz witnessed some members of staff being manoeuvred into positions where it seemed they could then be sacked. Liz felt that her disciplinary warning was the first step to her being replaced; it was the beginning of the witch-hunt. She thought that wasn't right and was determined to stand her ground and I fully supported her decision because I agreed with her that she was treated very badly indeed. I think if Charles had known he would have been horrified that his senior staff had given her a disciplinary warning during her maternity leave. Liz knew that the only option open to her was to treat it as unfair dismissal and go to a tribunal.

Unfortunately, she was forced to change solicitors at the preparatory stages when the original ones just cooled off, then dropped out; to this day, I have no idea why. Another solicitor stepped in, Stephen Venton, and he had to pick up the pieces very quickly.

As Liz was going through the case with him, she mentioned an instance where she was going through a policy and procedures document in the St James's Palace dining room and as she left the room she heard Fawcett utter a racist comment about her. She told the new solicitor that she had spoken to Amanda Yaxley, Highgrove's personnel officer, about the incident and had been told to make sure she had a witness. But I knew it would be virtually impossible for anyone to come forward because they were all too scared of losing their jobs, even though Liz was adamant that enough people had heard it for her to present a case. But it was brought up in the tribunal and, in hindsight, I think bringing up the issue of race was a mistake. The Prince's solicitor picked up on this and asked what she was focusing on, was it working conditions or race allegations? She was fighting on two fronts now and it was hard enough fighting on one. If she had stuck to her unfair dismissal claim without the racial allegations, then maybe the end result might have been different. But ultimately the tribunal ruled that she had failed to prove any of the allegations and she lost. It resulted in a lot of sleepless nights and much heartbreak and frustration. But there have been other tribunals since, so I feel that her taking a stand allowed others to come forward, even though she was bitterly disappointed.

CHAPTER FOURTEEN
IT'S GROUNDHOG DAY

By the end of my term as the Queen Mother's equerry, I had been on a journey that ninety-nine point nine per cent of the population would never experience. It was an amazing journey during which I met some fabulous people. But, and this is the crux, it was still a job and I wanted to move on. Others who had held the post and saw the whole thing as a series of social engagements that they were happy to be part of were sad to leave. But I was pleased to be escaping the fierce protocol – not necessarily that which surrounded the Queen Mother, because she had a habit of sometimes dispensing with real formality, but with the tedium of tasks such as letter writing, remembering the right way to address people, always wearing the right clothes and all sorts of little things that caught you unawares on an almost daily basis. To be perfectly frank, the protocol is one of the principal things I do not miss and it was perhaps the main reason I couldn't have done the job forever. There's only so much formality one person can take and, as with any job, the work of an equerry has its lifespan and after two years that's it. By the end, I really was looking forward to a fresh challenge. But the experience had affected me in certain ways and changed me slightly, though not as much as the people who had been at Clarence House for decades, and there were quite a few of them. They had become almost institutionalised –inextricably intertwined with the palace.

I found that although I hadn't changed in some ways – I still wore the same clothes and frequented the same pubs and wine bars as I had before I got the job – in others I had. I realised things about life by working at Clarence House, chiefly that I was in a situation where if someone less senior than the Queen Mother were trying to make me feel little or insignificant, they just appeared nonsensical now, and I did come across these bizarre situations when I left where I would be interviewed by the managing director of a company, who was trying to be overbearing and pompous, and I would find that I just wasn't fazed by the situation or him any more. The Royal Family had been so nice, and yet were so much more senior to anyone else, that if anyone else wasn't as nice as they were, that person just seemed silly to me. If I had been insecure about certain aspects of my life pre-Queen Mother, I certainly wasn't after it. I was a lot more self-assured and, if I ever encountered anyone being even remotely pompous, I just considered them slightly strange.

The three-month handover was to a Sandhurst contemporary of mine called Charlie MacEwan. We knew each other very well – in fact, he was the main reason I decided to go into the Irish Guards in the first place. This meant that the 'training' period he had to go through under me was reasonably light-hearted and I could explain things to him fairly candidly. It was enormous fun to facilitate the process of turning someone from an outsider to an insider. Having spent many years doing regular Army duties with Charlie, including operational tours in Central America, Germany and Northern Ireland, it was quite easy to be able to explain to him the subtle arts of directional talking, gauging the mood of guests and generally anticipating what the Queen Mother would need. However, I soon discovered that words like 'training' and 'induction' didn't really apply because it was like trying to explain the inexplicable, but he understood it, kind of, and I found that the way he operated was similar to me in many ways. He, like me, just picked up the etiquette and protocol he had learned in the Army and applied it to the Clarence House routine, and the Queen Mother treated him in exactly the same way as she had done with all her previous equerries and took the changeover in her stride. Charlie reacted to the job in the same way I had when I started. I remember telling him about the intricacies of directional talking and him just staring at me wide-eyed and mouthing, 'Oh my life, this is bizarre.'

I would explain the various changes of outfit at different times for different occasions and he would look at me quizzically and say: 'But why do you have to wear that?'

And I would be thinking, why exactly? All I could tell him was: 'Because you do, you just do. I can't really explain why, it's just something that's expected of you'.

Ninety per cent of the induction period was spent showing him the correct way to write letters and the correct way to address people, that sort of thing. As he came from a similar military background to me and was in the same regiment, this sort of protocol came quite easily to him, as it generally did with all the equerries because it was rare for the Household to choose anyone who was inappropriate.

Eventually, the time came for me to leave and say my goodbyes and I remember the Queen Mother saying, 'I'm sad to see you go but you must keep in touch.'

This was a touching little comment and she may well have been sad but there was no great emotion on her part. It was just a statement; she had probably said the same thing to all the other equerries. There was no crying or hugs or anything like that. She said things to me such as, 'I hope you'll come back for lunches from time to time,' and obviously there was no way I was going to turn down that offer. Cufflinks were a standard leaving present for the equerries. All the previous equerries had received them and sure enough the Queen Mother handed me a small leather case containing cufflinks for me.

But to me, possibly the most valuable thing that the Queen Mother gave me at that time had the least commercial value – the Post-it note with Churchill's battle cry.

I had every intention of going back and did, as did many other former equerries, apart from the ones who had started new lives in a different country, obviously. I remember one equerry who had left the Army and gone gold mining. He was living a kind of H. Rider Haggard sort of life, and from time to time he would surface back in Britain and pop in to see the Queen Mother, bringing with him a gold nugget for her to look at. She found this fascinating and, would spend the whole lunch quizzing him about his adventures in countries such as South Africa and the neighbouring provinces. She wanted to know everything about his life since he had been her equerry, as she did with most of the others who were invited for lunch.

The ones who left Clarence House to work in the City came quite often and those visits were the easiest for me to organise because when they came they knew all the staff very well and just got straight involved with the lunch, and even chipped in with helping. It was almost as if they had got their job back for the afternoon because they knew the routine inside out. They would arrive and, if there were any other guests present, visiting MPs or Army types, they would help to look after them, pouring them drinks and making them feel at home. Moments like these made my job blissfully easy because I noticed a kind of pulling together between me and any ex-equerry who turned up. It was as though there was a kind of solidarity between us and we quickly built an affinity because they knew that they had had to deal with the same issues as I did when they worked there, so they wanted to do their best to make my job that day as easy as possible.

It was the same with issues of protocol and etiquette. If I didn't know something and needed to get advice without going to Ralph or Alastair, I would telephone an ex-equerry for help or, alternatively, I would consult what was known as the Blue Book. This was like an A–Z listing of all the issues and points of protocol that would come into an equerry's sphere of operation. It was really the only handover document that existed for the equerries, and for such a simple item, it was indispensable as it had been updated over many years by all the predecessors. The hints and tips inside ranged from trips to Aberdeen Airport to zoo visits; you name it, and there was a very good chance it would be in there. It listed all the things the Queen Mother had done and the places she had been to in alphabetical order. For example, if I wanted to know what the protocol was for a particular lunch, I would look in the Blue Book under the subject matter and, hopefully, previous equerries would have listed the points of protocol and etiquette for it. There was a whole host of tips and advice in it: advice on when to sit down at certain functions; how to keep the conversation flowing at a certain event; what to wear during visits and State occasions – a whole cornucopia of things.

I remember browsing through it in the early days and coming across some rather obvious advice, such as always serve drinks to all the guests before serving yourself, and always, always serve the Queen Mother first. There had been tips that had gone by the wayside. Many years earlier it had been standard etiquette always to stop eating when a member of the Royal Family put his or her knife and fork down to signal that they had finished their meal, and you did this even if you hadn't completed yours. The Queen Mother had ditched this tradition many years ago. She ate so little that I think she imagined people would starve if they followed that rule. Other notes advised that the Queen Mother wasn't keen on fish that hadn't been filleted and had bones in it, and under 'Wine', someone had written that she preferred red to white. There were other snippets, such as don't press the bell to summon a servant in the Queen Mother's presence, unless she has invited you to do it, or when to wear dress shirts, when to wear a stiff collar and when not to wear one. The Blue Book was full of little things that were vital to understanding the job. And most importantly, the book contained little caveats and personal comments from the previous equerries on interesting places to go and visit while on tour.

One of the notes included tips on how to gain short-term membership of the Craigendarroch Country Club near Balmoral in Scotland. This was a useful bolthole on occasional afternoons off, where you could go swimming or be thrashed at squash by one of the royal bodyguards. I added quite a lot of things to it myself. I remember there being no notes on the RAF Club in London, so after we had been there on a visit, I came back, opened up the book and started a new section under R for RAF Club and noted that the place had a strange positioning of the loos. I also noted that the lift was absolutely tiny so I advised my successors to avoid using the lift if in the company of more than three guests. For our visit to the *Ark Royal*, I made notes about the protocol involved in visiting Navy ships and the best practices once on board.

If I needed to know a point of protocol or etiquette and it wasn't in the Blue Book, I would find out about it from an ex or present member of staff before making a note in the book for future reference. It proved invaluable as an operational manual. But if I was really stuck, I generally telephoned my predecessor Edward Dawson-Daimer. He was a pretty good font of knowledge and was very useful in pulling me out of a hole; they all were in their own way. If I had to do a timings list for a particular visit, I could often look at one done for a similar event by my predecessor and that would give me all the information I needed in terms of who I should call and, at the places we would be visiting who I needed to brief. But if there was one person I relied on more than anyone, it was James Patrick, the outgoing Queen's equerry. He was handy because he was so easy to get in touch with and because he had been working at Buckingham Palace much longer than I had at Clarence House. The Queen's equerry was a three-year posting rather than my two-year one and James was just handing over to his successor, Royal Navy Commander Toby Williamson. I would very often ask him about protocol, such as how to address an Earl. I remember him telling me never to teach a Duchess how to curtsey because they should really know, and to simply ask, 'Are you happy with what you are doing?' when going through the procedures in meeting the Queen Mother. This gave visitors an easy and guilt-free opportunity to ask a question if they weren't certain about something.

If it all seems like a bit of a minefield, that's probably because it was. My standard questions to other equerries would be along the lines of: 'How do I explain this to people?' or 'How can I get round this particular problem in terms of the correct protocol?'

I remember, not long after I started the job, asking a former equerry 'Are you allowed to say if you want to go for a pee during lunch?'

He told me I could go for a pee, but that I would have to be as discreet as possible and use the entrance the servants used, rather than the main door used by the Queen Mother and her home team.

Letter writing was an art in itself and to get the correct terminology was crucial. For example, a letter to an Admiral would be addressed differently from, say, a letter to the Lord Chancellor. This was one of the most important things to get right as equerry because you were constantly writing letters and you had to get them right as you were writing on behalf of the Queen Mother.

For formal letters to the Queen Mother, the protocol would be to sign off with 'I have the honour to be, Ma'am, your obedient Servant'. Formal letters to the Queen are signed off in the same manner, only changing 'Servant' to 'Subject'.

I found the job difficult only in the sense that I couldn't afford to make mistakes because these were immediately picked up on by all the staff. The employees hardly ever made mistakes at Clarence House and everybody self-consciously knew that they had to be 100 per cent perfect in their role. If anyone tripped up, they tended to trip up not on the big things, because you could get help for them, but on smaller matters. For example, organising big visits was not that difficult and not that stressful. It was the little things that happened on a moment to moment basis, such as remembering to bow at the right times and remembering to pour the Queen Mother's drink before you made anyone else's. These were the things that most people would consider quite trivial which could easily catch you out.

An organisation like the Army thrives on what has been termed 'bull' – short for bullshit – that is, things such as polishing your shoes and your brass buttons until they gleam, standing to attention at the right moments, and saluting the appropriate rank – the little things that get you regimented, organised, and always thinking and on your toes. There was less bull at Clarence House than in the Army but it did exist, mainly through Ralph, and really in order to keep you constantly alert. But at least at Clarence House you felt that it was done largely through respect for the Queen Mother. I wouldn't really think about it in normal life. It did trip me up sometimes and I remember being told by a member of staff: 'The Queen Mother would like to see you straight away about a letter she wants to send someone.'

It sounded pretty urgent so I hurried in to her a little too rushed and forgot to bow. This wasn't a major problem – especially if you were in and out of the room on a regular basis – after a while a cursory nod of the head would suffice. But normally I was okay and swam with the tide.

This was opposed to somebody like Ralph, who really never made mistakes of any kind – well, not knowingly. Obviously, when he got older and his health suffered, he would occasionally fall asleep at lunch but that was not a mistake because the Queen Mother didn't see it as a problem. People at Clarence House generally didn't cock up. The clock-winder came in at exactly the same time every week and you could set your watch on William's and Reg's routine. However, they were emotionally driven professionals and the Queen Mother would occasionally detect if they were in a bad mood; they might be curt to another member of staff or something and when they had left the room she would say something like, 'Oh, just ignore them. They're a bit upset because the trip has gone on for two days longer than it should.'

The Queen Mother she had this amazingly ability to read people's moods, and she had the uncanny knack of knowing at all times what everybody was thinking, even though she never got emotionally involved herself. She would throw the anger and distress at whomever she was talking to and let them deal with it.

The job of equerry is rather like being a swan. A swan seems to glide across the water effortlessly yet under the surface its feet are paddling around like a lunatic to get it where it wants to go. It was quite hard juggling all my tasks, trying to understand protocol and procedure and getting things organised while maintaining this calm façade.

By the time my final week came, I had already handed over most of the job to Charlie and there really wasn't a lot of work for me to do, save to ring round and tell the people who needed to know who the new equerry was and just generally say my goodbyes. There were a lot of fond farewells but never really any sort of final goodbyes because I was always told, 'Well, we'll see you soon for lunch when you pop in.' So everybody was expecting me to come back and see the Queen Mother from time to time and not just fade away into a new life.

My handover was great. I was happy to be handing over to Charlie who was 100 per cent competent. If he hadn't been, it would have reflected badly on me because I was the one who had to train him for three months. So I knew I simply had to get him fully versed in every aspect of the job. But fortunately, after about three or four weeks of handover, he got the gist of it and virtually assumed the role full time. I then found myself almost switching into a position similar to the one occupied by Ralph, in as much as I would be constantly throwing Charlie little hints and tips, such as, 'Remember, at lunch, don't have seconds unless the Queen Mother does,' and all sorts of things that I had picked up myself over the two years.

My last day, which was a Friday, was when I got my cufflinks and the Post-it note, and I spent most of it going round different offices not saying goodbye to people but saying 'See you when I'm back for lunch in a few months' time.'

The Queen Mother had left early to go to Royal Lodge for the weekend, as she always did on Fridays, and before she left at around 3.30 in the afternoon, she said to me, 'Thank you very much, Colin, for all your help over the last couple of years,' and that was that, off she went.

Everything, even down to my final departure, was conducted in a very businesslike and formal way because that was the way things were. Later that evening, I went out for dinner with friends; I suppose you could call it a leaving party of sorts, but there was nobody from Clarence House there. I felt it was yet another changing point in my life and once out of the Royal Household, I had some very important decisions to make regarding career options. I was twenty-eight and time wasn't going to wait for me, so I had to make up my mind fairly quickly. I had toyed with the idea of going back into the Army but throughout my life I had always been very interested in the media and the thought of going into something like television and film production excited me immensely, so I made the decision that that was what I would do. I was going to change my life completely and leave the Army.

I arranged to go on a BBC presenter's course and began to learn the basics of television production through BBC courses, books and computer programmes. Then I fired off a few CVs to various people. I soon discovered that sticking 'Queen Mother's Equerry' in as one of my previous jobs on my CV could be something of a double-edged sword. Some of my friends and colleagues told me it would open doors for me, but I found that some potential employers would look at it and not quite believe what they were reading. They honestly thought that I was joking, and it wasn't that big a selling point anyway for television. So I played it down on my CV and only touched on it during interviews, telling my interviewer that the job entailed looking after someone at a very senior level and organising high-profile events and visits down to the tiniest details. That was how I pitched it to them and I could tell which employers were pro-royal and which were anti-royal by their reaction to the job.

While all this was going on, I was back at Pirbright with the Irish Guards as a Support Company Commander. This was a specialist company that looked after things like heavy machine guns and anti-tank missiles, and I had about 120 soldiers under my command. It all felt a bit surreal going from flying with the Army to working for the Queen Mother and back into the Army again, but because I knew I would be leaving, I didn't feel that I was getting stuck in a rut. My role had also changed slightly. Since I had experience as an equerry, I was used more as an organiser of things like VIP visits, ceremonial dinners and the like. They basically used the experience I had garnered at Clarence House. I remember organising the visit to Pirbright of the regimental colonel, who was the Grand Duke of Luxembourg. He came over for St Patrick's Day and I was entrusted with organising the whole thing and making sure the right people were invited from the palace. Jobs like that worked out quite nicely for me because they were quite easy after two years at Clarence House, and in a way it felt like I had my old job back. I stayed at Pirbright for two months, but I was desperate to leave the Army and it was the right time for me to go. Flying helicopters had been very exciting but there were very few things left that I wanted to do. And of course, ultimately, the Army is about warfare.

I had joined the Army when the Cold War was still on and protecting the country seemed a worthwhile job; policing trouble spots around the world somehow seemed less appealing. I wanted to change direction and wanted to go into a more creative industry. I had enjoyed the job, but after having worked for the Queen Mother, I was a different person, and the thought of going to places like Iraq and fighting on the frontline just didn't excite me anymore. I also found that people's reactions to me differed. Soldiers would see my pilot's wings and also know that I had looked after the Queen Mother and to them it was an odd combination and one they couldn't really comprehend. They would be a little more deferential because there was a slight mystique surrounding working for a member of the Royal Family; it really did feel quite strange. Since no one outside the royal residences could ever really know what it was like inside, there was an intrigue about the job as equerry. I was also allowed to keep the rank of major which was a pleasant surprise. But most of all, there had been a lot of changes in personnel in the regiment. With my flying tour and my job with the Queen Mother, I had been away from the Irish Guards for nearly six years. In that time, many officers had joined and left without my even knowing them.

Within a few months of going back to the Army, I left to join a communications company called Merlin which specialised in corporate videos. The job entailed selling off existing training videos to local authorities. It sounds boring, but the reality was much, much worse. Even so, it was my first step on the ladder to television and film production and I was being groomed to be their sales manager for all their training videos. I got to grips with the job pretty quickly, certainly quickly enough to work out that I didn't want to be in sales, which didn't appeal to me on a creative level. So I stuck it out while looking for new opportunities in production and film-making. I realised that in order for things to change, I had to change them. Rather than simply selling existing films to different local councils, I suggested that we might make a new one for them. Eventually, one council went for it and I asked my MD if I could get involved with making it.

Fortunately, he told me to go ahead and I was finally producing my own videos. I was editing one at the ITV Television Centre in Bristol when I got chatting to a bloke who turned out to be the head of production for ITV West. He asked me about my life and I told him that I had worked for the Queen Mother and gave him my Army background. When I told him that I was in aviation, his eyes lit up. Wingspan Air & Space Channel, who are the makers of the Discovery *Wings* series, were looking for someone with flying knowledge to make programmes for cable television. He almost offered me the job on the spot and before I knew it I was in Washington for an interview. Less than two months later, I was tasked with building the UK branch of the channel, which was something that my Army background helped me with, because I was able to source expertise to get things built. I worked with a *Sky News* producer, Adam Brown, to set up a 'news and documentary' team in Bristol and less than six months later I was making news and documentaries to be sold to the Discovery Channel and other cable outlets, which was great. I had finally found my true vocation in life and it felt fantastic.

People used to ask me how a life as an Army officer could have possibly prepared me for a life in television, and I simply said, 'What, you mean get a group of people to a country with the right equipment, do a job without getting them killed and get them back again. What do you think?' and just smiled. Okay, it was a bit dramatic, but basically right.

While all this was going on, it never felt strange to be away from Clarence House because since I was only there for two years I wasn't really institutionalised by the place. I always felt when I left that I was going back to the normal world, but I was invited back for lunch after just a couple of months away when Alastair called and said, 'The Queen Mother is having lunch. Would you like to come because she will be interested to find out how you are getting on?'

It came as a nice surprise to be invited so soon after leaving, but when Alastair said the Queen Mother would like to know how I was getting on, all I could think was that they must be thin on the ground for lunch guests on that particular day as I had made exactly the same calls to other equerries when there was a shortage of guests during my time there. Alastair would tell me to see who I could muster up and I would do the usual ringing round to the regular crowd. But it dawned on me when he rang that I had now gone from being equerry to being part of the regular crowd of ex-equerries, like Ashe Wyndham, who could always be relied upon to turn up to any Queen Mother event at a moment's notice. I had to accept the invitation; after all, if anyone were invited to see the Queen for lunch they would hardly turn it down, would they? I also knew that by accepting I had become part of the solution, rather than the problem, and I could help out with the drinks and so forth. So it was a good thing, and anyway, I have this philosophy in life that you should never turn down invitations to parties and lunches because you never know what opportunities will be presented once you're there. If you turned down lunch with the Queen Mother, you might only get two more invitations. Turn these down and you would be off the invitation list. I found it an honour still to be asked and it was a privilege after my employment there had finished.

When I walked through the door of Clarence House as a guest rather than a worker, it was the strangest feeling I have ever had, mainly because it was like going back in time to being the equerry again. It was as if nothing had changed and I felt as thought I had been away for ten minutes rather than two months. It was like that every time I went back, which was every few months for the next six years. Nothing ever changed. It was the most peculiar thing I have ever come across in my life. The Queen Mother greeted me with, 'Ah, Colin, how are you? Have a drink and tell me everything.'

This was exactly the same way she had greeted me as her equerry. To her, I had done nothing more than step out of the room and step back in again minutes later. It's like when very close friends meet after a period apart. They don't jabber on about what they have been doing while they haven't seen each other; they just get on talking about the issues of the day as though they have never parted company, and this was what it was like with the Queen Mother. On my first visit back, I had lunch and managed to pick up on the fact that now, as a guest rather than employee, the job really did seem to consume the equerry.

I could observe him from a distance and note that he was completely immersed in the role, making sure everything was right and that the guests were entertained, and he had to ensure at all times that things were running smoothly. I felt relieved not to be up to my neck in protocol anymore after watching him.

After lunch, I went round some of the offices, saying hello to the various secretaries, butlers and kitchen staff. I even got the impression from some of the older members of staff that they thought I had been out of their life for only a few minutes. One member of the kitchen staff even said to me, 'Are you making a lunch request?' Then he quickly corrected himself and said, 'Oh, God, you left a couple of months ago, didn't you?'

It was then that I got the impression that some of the people there really had lost their grip on time and events. They had become totally immersed in Clarence House and everything that went with it to the detriment of their lives outside its walls. Time really had stood still for a lot of people, especially the Queen Mother, who, by then, was very much a woman of routine and predictability, as most old people are. Ralph was no different. He gave me the once-over when I stepped through the door to make sure I had given my shoes a good polish and that my shirt was properly ironed, which they were. The only change this time was that I wore a regular shirt collar rather than a starched one, and Ralph noticed this and said, 'I see you are in casual clothing.'

In fact, I was wearing the best shirt and tie I had, but I was relieved that Ralph had welcomed me back in this way; it proved he still had his wits about him and that there was still some sharpness there.

But I don't think I can emphasise enough when I say that nothing had changed. It was spooky. The same works of art were on the walls – the Queen Mother was very into twentieth-century pieces by John Piper, Graham Sutherland, W. S. Sickert and Augustus John to name but a few – and there was still her amazing Fabergé collection, her collection of English porcelain, plus the silver and legacies from the Bowes Lyon family. They were in exactly the same places as they had been when I left. I felt at certain points a strong sense of *déjà vu*. It became quite disconcerting and every time I went back for lunch I would leave feeling a bit perturbed and ask myself why nothing ever changed. At some stage in the Queen Mother's life, she must have gone into a kind of *Groundhog Day* mode. But at what point did she do this? I suspect her routine evolved slowly from the moment the King died, but that's just a guess.

What I do know is that the staff who had been there for over thirty years told me that the routine was the same one that had been going on for decades, and I saw no noticeable changes even after I left, not a single one. Even four years after I had gone, the décor was the same, the senior staff members hadn't changed, and she still drank her gin and Dubonnet at the magic hour, got up at the same time, and watched *Fawlty Towers* and *Keeping Up Appearances*. I cannot put my finger on anything that was different. At least when you go and visit your parents, or even your old school, there is a sense that things have changed a little, but I have never met anyone else who made me feel that their world has been exactly the same as it was some thirty years previously. She had a timeless quality about her and she didn't seem any older or worse healthwise, though she would never let on anyway if she were feeling unwell. She epitomised what the Royal Family was all about. They carried on regardless of what was going on around them in the outside world, and the Queen Mother was happy in her own little world and more or less oblivious to world events going on about her because she had lived through so many and been at the centre of them for so long that she just couldn't be bothered anymore. Her life was the way she wanted it. It was predictable, it was orderly and she had her routines. She had become almost immortal with an enduring quality about her.

The only changes were with the staff that came and went. A chap called Patrick Kyle was her accountant and his health deteriorated, but in spite of this, he soldiered on. He had joined the household in the seventies from Coutts bank on an understanding he gave to his wife that it was to be his last job and that he would do it for ten years before retiring. By 1997, his wife was saying to him, 'Please retire. Why can't you retire?'

But the feeling among the senior staff was, how could they retire when their employer was some twenty years older than they and working flat out seven days a week? It just didn't seem right to these people, so they stayed; then various members of staff suffered heart attacks, strokes, angina attacks or other ailments, yet they still ploughed on. While the Queen Mother always seemed to be as fit as a fiddle, everyone around her seemed to be dropping like flies. Ralph was a typical example. His health really did deteriorate after I left and he would come in on a Sunday thinking it was Monday, or ask people where certain folders were that didn't actually exist. Fortunately, I always seemed to come on his good days, when he could at least recognise me. He was suffering from some sort of progressive dementia and it was heartbreaking to see his gradual decline.

In complete contrast, the Queen Mother appeared well right up until the day she died. She was mentally sound, fully aware and fully functioning at all times. When I turned up for the job, I had people coming to me from my Army regiment saying that I would be the last equerry to work for her because she was so old. I told this to my predecessor and he said that he had been told the same thing by the equerry before him and he added, 'You know what? The last ten equerries have all been told that they would be the last one.'

So I said to my successor, 'She's going to outlive us all, Charlie.'

She often pointed out some of the frailer older guests and said to me, 'Oh well, you have to look after them. They're getting on a bit,' or 'They are eighty, they are quite old, so best look after them carefully.'

I was thinking, crumbs, you're ninety-six! It's hard to

believe that she is dead now because she was such an ingrained part of many people's lives, which is why she acquired the reputation she did as a national treasure. People could rely on her being exactly the same at all times. They knew that she would never act inappropriately, say the wrong thing or ever be out of character. When Elizabeth Bowes Lyon became the Queen Mother, the clock stopped and she became the most consistent Royal in history.

Epilogue

The phone rang at 3.00 in the morning and my wife Elizabeth picked it up: 'Hello, Elizabeth. It's St James's Palace. Princess Diana's been involved in a car accident in Paris. She's injured. Just letting you know in case anybody tries to contact you about it.'

'How bad is it?' Liz asked.

'It's too early to say, but we'll keep you informed.'

Liz woke me up to tell me. 'Ah well,' I said, 'I'm sure she'll get the best medical attention there is,' and with that I drifted back to sleep.

A few hours later, the telephone rang again. Liz picked it up and said, 'Oh my God.'

Turning to me she mouthed the words 'Diana's died'. I was completely shocked. I couldn't believe something like that had happened. It was almost like a member of my family had gone. I had met and chatted to her and it really affected me. This was a person I knew.

Liz was called in to St James's Palace that morning to deal with the deluge of flowers and cards that were arriving by the bucket load. It was all hands on deck because the nation had gone into collective mourning the like of which had never been seen before. I was a bit out of it by then because I was working in television production, but I followed it on television and in the newspapers, and Liz kept me up to date with what was happening at the Palace. She said the Royal Family had been put under tremendous strain and immense pressure, and many people seemed to be blaming them for Diana's death, and the whole situation was beginning to run away from them with events conspiring to paint the Monarchy in the worst possible light. It was a crisis of monumental proportions. Personally, I couldn't believe some people's reactions to Diana's death.

The Royals came in for all sorts of criticism, mainly because they hadn't shown a public display of emotion in the days following the tragedy. I just thought this was wrong. You can't criticise the way someone shows their grief because it is such a deeply personal thing. Everyone handles bereavement differently, and the manner in which the members of the Royal Family show their grief is a matter for them alone. Death is the final sanctuary, and if someone close to you dies, you have to be left alone, not attacked. The whole thing was deeply wrong.

I didn't see the Queen Mother until a couple of months after the event and it never came up in conversation because

Diana's name was never mentioned at Clarence House. I don't think the Queen Mother ever uttered Diana's name, nor talked about her ever again, once she split from Charles. The Royal Family had a tendency just to get on with it and make the best out of a bad situation. They have always done well at soldiering on and that is what they did.

Soldiering on is what the Queen Mother did best. But as the years went on it was becoming obvious that, to paraphrase the words of Andrew Marvell, 'Time's winged chariot was drawing near'. There was no real slowdown in the Queen Mother's mental faculties, nor any marked deterioration in her health; she just didn't have the stamina to endure the daily ritual of lunches with guests any more. I found that invitations to Clarence House were becoming more infrequent and my last visit came in 2001, a year before she died. I didn't notice any great change in her. She was still laughing and joking and was in quite good form. I remember saying to her equerry, 'She's never going to stop. She's just going to keep going on and on.'

But she did stop, and it wasn't really a winding down. She just kept going and then stopped. She slipped away peacefully at 3.15 pm on Saturday 30 March 2002.

It's hard to say how I felt at that moment. Is it a big shock when someone aged nearly 102 years old dies? Well, yes and no. It wasn't really a surprise because we all knew the day would come, but on the other hand there was a feeling of shock because the day really had come when she had gone and I felt waves of huge sadness, more so than when Diana died because I was not that connected to the Princess.

I spoke to a few old colleagues at Clarence House; they were making preparations for her funeral and had taken on extra staff to cope with the huge influx of flowers and gifts that were again pouring in. By this time, the Royal Family had become quite familiar with funerals because Princess Margaret had died only a few weeks earlier. The team at Clarence House remained there for some months after the Queen Mother's funeral sorting out the gifts and handling the running down of her administration.

The funeral itself was awe-inspiring and on a par with Winston Churchill's. It took place on Tuesday 9 April at Westminster Abbey. I remember hearing nothing but the sound of bagpipes as the procession moved from Westminster Hall to the Abbey and it brought a lump to my throat. What struck me most on a personal level was that I had worked for this woman and when you work for someone for so long you see them as a person, with all their traits brought to the fore. Yet, at the funeral, it was suddenly brought home to me exactly who I had worked for. This was a woman whose impact on the world had been enormous and that was what struck me at her funeral. I kept thinking that this was a former Queen of England and it had been an honour for me to have been associated with her. I realised the full weight of her position in the world as a great icon of the twentieth century. I had never really experienced the full whack of pomp and ceremony during my time as equerry because there wasn't much of it in the Queen Mother's world towards the end of her life; it was all very domestic when

I worked for her, so this extraordinary funeral was quite a jolt to the senses.

Inside the Abbey, I was seated with past and present members of the Queen Mother's staff. They all seemed okay and generally nobody looked overcome. People had been prepared for this moment for years. Although there was sadness and emotion, it was nothing like the wailing that preceded Diana's funeral. With Diana there had been a lot of people who didn't know anything about her or have any concept of what the Royal Family was about; they just fell for the whole fairy-tale concept. But with the Queen Mother it was totally different.

There was a sense of great historical importance surrounding the event that made the degree of sadness totally different from that felt for Diana. It was a much more meaningful grief for the Queen Mother because she had a longer track record. Older people felt more moved by her death than they had done by Diana's because they had lived through everything she had lived through and, in the case of World War II, had suffered as she had suffered during the bombings and rationing. The whole event was much more respectful, conservative and heartfelt. Diana's death was more of a tragedy; it was the cutting short of a life. You could hardly say that about the Queen Mother. Her funeral was a mixture of sadness and an appreciation of her life.

I found it most interesting at the Queen Mother's funeral that all the government ministers and heads of state were seated very close to the front of the Abbey, while all the Queen Mother's domestic staff (including me) and the people who knew her best were tucked at the back of the Abbey. On a human level it was sad, but it was also understandable. Although all the people who knew her best were farthest away, in terms of protocol for this kind of event it was the right thing to do. But it was sad to see people like William Tallon – people who had worked all their life for the Queen Mother – almost left out of the proceedings, and I know that Prince Philip, of all people, noticed this and complained about it afterwards. But the Queen Mother would probably have said it was the right thing to do.

Throughout the ceremony there was a friendly atmosphere pervading the place and a feeling of amazement that this woman really had had a good innings. A lot of people reminisced and told stories about her. I spoke to a guy from a press organisation before the service began and he told me how he had reported on a military event years ago at which the Queen Mother was a guest and how there were a few hundred people in attendance, and he said, 'You know, she spoke to every single person in the room on a one-to-one basis for at least a couple of minutes. I couldn't believe it. Everybody was just thrilled and there was a real buzz about the place when she left.'

I remember coming out of the service and people were standing in Parliament Square all waiting for a copy of the order of service. They just wanted to be part of the whole thing. It was a nice celebration of her life rather than the mourning of a death. I had received an invitation to go back to Clarence House after the service, but I couldn't make it, and anyway, the place wouldn't have been the same without the Queen Mother there. So that was that. Everybody just drifted away and a major chapter of my life had closed, leaving me nothing but warm memories of a woman who was the epitome of old-fashioned values, and by that I don't just mean a sense of correctness in terms of etiquette and protocol, but also an old-fashioned love of life – similar to Noel Coward's well-known breeziness about life and enjoyment of its little quirks and foibles. She had an innocence about her that manifested itself in an easiness and comfort with almost everybody she met and which seemed to affect them deeply on a personal level. The thing that meant the most to me about the Queen Mother was how much she cared about people. She was an inspiration. I have no doubt that history will be kind to her. She was the greatest of ambassadors of a forgotten age.

SOURCES

The author expresses his indebtedness to the following books and articles, which have been studied for the purposes of this publication:

Elizabeth the Queen Mother, Hugo Vickers, Hutchison, London, 2005

'Pink Gins, Family Secrets And A Butler Who Fell Out Of A Lift…My Hilarious Lunch With The QM' by Tim Heald, the *Daily Mail* 2002

'Another World' presented by Don Murray, CBC News Analysis, 6 November 2000

'Highgrove Secretary Claims Racial Abuse by Prince Charles' Staff' by Stephen Bates, the *Guardian*, 7 December 2001

'Prince's Former Secretary Loses Racial Discrimination

Case' by Stephen Bates, the *Guardian*, 8 December 2001

'A Wicked Twinkle and a Streak of Steel' by Lucy Moore, the *Observer*, 31 March 2002

Major Sir Ralph Hugo Anstruther (Obituary), the *Daily Telegraph*, 22 May 2002

'Charles' Aide Gets Job With Royal Food Firm' by David Rowe, *Sunday Mirror*, 9 March 2003

'The Diana Tape: "Charles Is Too Close" to Fawcett' by Alan Rimmer and Rupert Hamer, *Sunday Mirror*, 16 March 2003

'Revealed: Secrets of the "Rape Tape"' by James Saville, *Sunday Mirror*, 2 November 2003

'Alone At Last (With Just A Few House Guests)' by Elizabeth Grice, the *Daily Telegraph*, 9 April 2005

'A Brideshead Hideaway for Princesses At War' by Ben Fenton, the *Daily Telegraph*, 10 January 2006

www.castleofmey.org.uk

www.cnn.com ('Tributes Pour In For The Queen Mum', 22 April 2002)

www.horseracing.about.com

www.royal.gov.uk

www.wikipedia.org